WOMAN'S TRIALS

OR,

TALES AND SKETCHES FROM THE LIFE AROUND US

T. S. ARTHUR

1st WORLD
LIBRARY
Literary Society

Woman's Trials

T. S. Arthur

© 1st World Library, 2006
PO Box 2211
Fairfield, IA 52556
www.1stworldlibrary.com
First Edition

LCCN: 2006907739

Softcover ISBN: 1-4218-2456-6
Hardcover ISBN: 1-4218-2356-X
eBook ISBN: 1-4218-2556-2

Purchase *"Woman's Trials"*
as a traditional bound book at:
www.1stWorldLibrary.com/purchase.asp?ISBN=1-4218-2456-6

1st World Library is a literary, educational organization
dedicated to:

- Creating a free internet library of downloadable ebooks

- Hosting writing competitions and offering book
publishing scholarships.

Interested in more 1st World Library books?
contact: literacy@1stworldlibrary.com
Check us out at: www.1stworldlibrary.com

1ˢᵗ World Library Literary Society

Giving Back to the World

"If you want to work on the core problem, it's early school literacy."

- James Barksdale, former CEO of Netscape

"No skill is more crucial to the future of a child, or to a democratic and prosperous society, than literacy."

- Los Angeles Times

Literacy... means far more than learning how to read and write... The aim is to transmit... knowledge and promote social participation."

- UNESCO

"Literacy is not a luxury, it is a right and a responsibility. If our world is to meet the challenges of the twenty-first century we must harness the energy and creativity of all our citizens."

- President Bill Clinton

"Parents should be encouraged to read to their children, and teachers should be equipped with all available techniques for teaching literacy, so the varying needs and capacities of individual kids can be taken into account."

- Hugh Mackay

PREFACE

THE title of this volume sufficiently indicates its purpose. The stories of which it is composed have been mainly written with the end of creating for woman, in the various life-trials through which she has to pass, sympathy and true consideration, as well in her own sex as in ours. We are all too much engrossed in what concerns ourselves - in our own peculiar wants, trials, and sufferings - to give that thought to others which true humanity should inspire. To the creator of fictitious histories is, therefore, left the task of reminding us of our duty, by presenting pictures from the world of life around us - moving pictures, in which we may not only see the effect of our actions upon others, but also the relations of others to society, and thus learn to sympathize with the tried and the tempted, the suffering and the oppressed, the grief-stricken and the mourner. It is good for us, at times, to forget ourselves; to think of others and feel a heart-warm interest in all that concerns them. If the perusal of this volume has such an effect upon the reader's mind, it will accomplish all that its author desires; for right feeling is but the prompter to right action.

This book is to be followed, immediately, by other volumes, to the number of twelve, printed in uniform style: the series, when complete, to be called, "ARTHUR'S LIBRARY FOR THE HOUSEHOLD."

"MARRIED LIFE," the volume to come after this, is passing through the press, and will be ready for publication in a few days.

CONTENTS

A LESSON OF PATIENCE

I WAS very unhappy, from a variety of causes, definable and undefinable. My chambermaid had been cross for a week, and, by talking to my cook, had made her dissatis-fied with her place. The mother of five little children, I felt that I had a weight of care and responsibility greater than I could support. I was unequal to the task. My spirits fell under its bare contemplation. Then I had been disappointed in a seamstress, and my children were, as the saying is, "in rags." While brooding over these and other dishearte-ning circumstances, Netty, my chambermaid, opened the door of the room where I was sitting, (it was Monday morning,) and said -

"Harriet has just sent word that she is sick, and can't come to-day."

"Then you and Agnes will have to do the washing," I replied, in a fretful voice; this new source of trouble completely breaking me down.

"Indeed, ma'am," replied Netty, tossing her head and speaking with some pertness, "*I* can't do the washing. I didn't engage for any thing but chamber-work."

And so saying she left me to my own reflections. I must own to feeling exceedingly angry, and rose to ring the bell for Netty to return, in order to tell her that she could go to washing or leave the house, as best suited her fancy. But the sudden recollection of a somewhat similar collision with a former chamber-maid, in which I was worsted, and compelled to do my own chamber-work for a week, caused me to hesitate, and, finally, to sit down and indulge in a hearty fit of crying.

When my husband came home at dinnertime, things did not seem very pleasant for him, I must own. I had on a long, a very long face - much longer than it was when he went away in the morning.

"Still in trouble, I see, Jane," said he. "I wish you would try and take things a little more cheerfully. To be unhappy about what is not exactly agreeable doesn't help the matter any, but really makes it worse."

"If you had to contend with what I have to contend with, you wouldn't talk about things being *exactly agreeable,*" I replied to this. "It is easy enough to talk. I only wish you had a little of my trouble; you wouldn't think so lightly of it."

"What is the great trouble now, Jane?" said my husband, without being at all fretted with my unamiable temper. "Let us hear. Perhaps I can suggest a remedy."

"If you will get me a washerwoman, you will exceedingly oblige me," said I.

"Where is Harriet?" he asked.

"She is sick, or pretends to be, I don't know which."

"Perhaps she will be well enough to do your washing to-morrow," suggested my husband.

"Perhaps is a poor dependence."

I said this with a tartness that ill repaid my husband's effort to comfort me. I saw that he felt the unkindness of my manner, in the slight shade that passed over his face.

"Can't you get some one else to do your washing this week?"

I made no reply. The question was easily asked. After that, my husband was silent, - silent in that peculiar way that I understood, too well, as the effect of my words, or tones, or state of mind. Here was another cause for unhappiness, in the reflection that I had disturbed my husband's peace.

I am sure that I did not much look like a loving wife and mother as I presided at the dinner table that day. The children never seemed so restless and hard to manage; and I could not help speaking to them, every now and then, "as if I would take their heads off;" but to little good effect.

After my husband went away on finishing his dinner, I went to bed, and cried for more than half the afternoon. Oh! how wretched I felt! Life seemed an almost intolerable burden.

Then my mind grew more composed, and I tried to think about what was to be done. The necessity for having the clothes washed was absolute; and this roused me, at length, as the most pressing domestic duty, into thinking so earnestly, that I presently rang the bell for Netty, who came in her own good time.

"Tell Agnes that I want to see her," said I, not in a very good-natured way.

The effect was that Netty left the chamber without replying, and slammed the door hard after her, which mark of disrespect set my blood to boiling. In a little while my cook made her appearance.

"Agnes," said I, "do you know of any one that can get to do the washing this week?"

Agnes thought for a few moments, and then replied -

"There's a poor woman who lives near my mother's. I think she goes out to wash sometimes."

"I wish you would step round and see if she can't come here to-morrow."

Agnes said that she would do so.

"Tell her she must come," said I.

"Very well, ma'am."

And Agnes withdrew.

In an hour she tame back, and said that she had seen the woman, who promised to come.

"What is her name?" I asked.

"Mrs. Partridge," was answered.

"You think she won't disappoint me?"

"Oh, no, ma'am. I don't think Mrs. Partridge is the kind of a woman to promise and then disappoint a person."

It was some relief to think I was going to get my washing done; but the idea of having the ironing about all the week fretted my mind. And no sooner was this leading trouble set aside, than I began to worry about the children's clothes, and the prospect of losing my cook, who had managed my kitchen more to my satisfaction than any one had ever done before.

The promise for a pleasant hour at home was but little more flattering to my husband, when he returned in the evening, than it had been at dinner time. I was still in a sombre mood.

In the morning Mrs. Partridge came early and commenced the washing. There was something in this woman's appearance that interested me, and something in her face that reminded me of somebody I had seen before; but when and where I could not tell. Although her clothes were poor and faded, there was nothing common about her, and she struck me as being superior to her class. Several times during the morning I had to go into the kitchen where she was at work, and each time her appearance impressed me more and more. An emotion of pity arose in my bosom, as I saw her bending over the washing tub, and remembered that, for this hard labour during a whole day, the pay was to be but seventy-five cents. And yet there was an air of meek patience, if not contentment, in her face; while I, who had every thing from which I ought to have derived happiness, was dissatisfied and full of trouble. While in her presence I felt rebuked for my complaining spirit.

At dinner time Mrs. Partridge came to my room, and with a gentle, patient smile on her face, said -

"If you have no objections, ma'am, I would like to run home for a few minutes to nurse my baby and give the children something to eat. I'll make up the time."

"Go by all means," I replied, with an effort to speak calmly.

The woman turned, and went quickly away.

"Run home to nurse the baby and give the children something to eat!" The words went through and through me. So unexpected a request, revealing, as it did, the existence of such biting poverty in one who was evidently bearing her hard lot without a murmur, made me feel ashamed of myself for complaining at things which I ought to have borne with a cheerful spirit. I had a comfortable, in fact a luxurious, home, a kind and provident husband, and servants to do every thing in my house. There was no lack of the means for procuring every natural good I might reasonably desire. But, between the means and the attainment of the natural blessings I sought, there were many obstacles; and, instead of going to work in a cheerful, confident spirit to remove those obstacles, I suffered their interposition to make me unhappy; and not me alone, but my husband and all around me. But here was a poor woman, compelled to labour hard with her hands before she could obtain even the means for supplying nature's most pressing wants, doing her duty with an earnest, resigned, and hopeful spirit!

T.S. Arthur

"It is wicked in me to feel as I do," I could not help saying, as I made an effort to turn away from the picture that was before me.

When Mrs. Partridge came back, which was in about half an hour, I said to her -

"Did you find all safe at home?"

"Yes, ma'am, thank you," she answered cheerfully.

"How old is your baby?"

"Eleven months old, ma'am."

"Is your husband living?"

"No, ma'am; he died more than a year ago."

"How many children have you?"

"Four."

"All young?"

"Yes, ma'am. The oldest is only in her tenth year, but she is a good little girl, and takes care of the baby for me almost as well as a grown person. I don't know what I would do without her."

"But ain't you afraid to leave them all at home alone, for so long a time?"

"No, ma'am. Jane takes excellent care of them, and she is so kind that they will obey her as well as they do me. I don't know what in the world I would do without her.

I am certainly blessed in having so good a child."

"And only in her tenth year!" said I - the image of my Alice coming before my mind, with the thought of the little use she would be as a nurse and care-taker of her younger brothers and sisters.

"She is young, I know," returned the washerwoman - "too young to be confined down as much as she is. But then she is a very patient child, and knows that her mother has a great deal to do. I often wish it was easier for her; though, as it can't be helped, I don't let it fret me, for you know that would do no good."

"But how in the world, Mrs. Partridge," said I, "do you manage to provide for four children, and do for them at the same time?"

"I find it hard work," she replied; "and sometimes I feel discouraged for a little while; but by patience and perseverance I manage to get along."

Mrs. Partridge went to her washing, and I sat down in my comfortable room, having a servant in every department of my family, and ample means for the supply of every comfort and luxury I could reasonably desire.

"If she can get along by patience and perseverance," said I to myself, "it's a shame for me that I can't." Still, for all this, when I thought of losing my cook through the bad influence of Netty, the chambermaid, I felt worried; and thinking about this, and what I should do for another cook, and the trouble always attendant upon bringing a new domestic into the house, made me, after a while, feel almost as unhappy as before. It was not long before Netty came into my room, saying, as she did so -

"Mrs. Smith, what frock shall I put on Alice?"

"The one with a blue sprig," I replied.

"That's in the wash," was answered.

"In the wash!" said I, in a fretful tone. "How came it in the wash?"

"It was dirty."

"No, it wasn't any such thing. It would have done very well for her to put on as a change to-day and to-morrow."

"Well, ma'am, it's in the wash, and no help for it now," said Netty, quite pertly.

I was dreadfully provoked with her, and had it on my tongue to order her to leave my presence instantly. But I choked down my rising indignation.

"Take the red and white one, then," said I.

"The sleeve's nearly torn off of that. There isn't any one that she can wear except her white muslin."

"Oh dear! It's too bad! What shall I do? The children are all in rags and tatters!"

And in this style I fretted away for three or four minutes, while Netty stood waiting for my decision as to what Alice was to wear.

"Shall she put on the white muslin?" she at length asked.

"No, indeed! Certainly not! A pretty condition she'd have it in before night! Go and get me the red and white frock, and I will mend it. You aught to have told me it was torn this morning. You knew there was nothing for the child to put on ut this. I never saw such a set as you are!"

Netty flirted away, grumbling to herself. When she came in, she threw the frock into my lap with manner so insolent and provoking that I could hardly keep from breaking out upon her and rating her soundly. One thing that helped to restrain me was the recollection of sundry ebullitions of a like nature that had neither produced good effects nor left my mind in a state of much self-respect or tranquillity.

I repaired the torn sleeve, while Netty stood by. It was the work of but five minutes.

"Be sure," said I, as I handed the garment to Netty, "to see that one of Alice's frocks is ironed first thing to-morrow morning."

The girl heard, of course, but she made no answer. That was rather more of a condescension than she was willing to make just then.

Instead of thinking how easily the difficulty of the clean frock for Alice had been gotten over, I began fretting myself because I had not been able to procure a seamstress, although the children were "all in rags and tatters."

T.S. Arthur

"What is to be done?" I said, half crying, as I began to rock myself backward and forward in the great rocking-chair. "I am out of all heart." For an hour I continued to rock and fret myself, and then came to the desperate resolution to go to work and try what I could do with my own hands. But where was I to begin? What was I to take hold of first? All the children were in rags.

"Not one of them has a decent garment to his back," said I.

So, after worrying for a whole hour about what I should do, and where I should begin, I abandoned the idea of attempting any thing myself, in despair, and concluded the perplexing debate by taking another hearty crying-spell. The poor washerwoman was forgotten during most of this afternoon. My own troubles were too near the axis of vision, and shut out all other objects.

The dusky twilight had begun to fall, and I was still sitting idly in my chamber, and as unhappy as I could be. I felt completely discouraged. How *was* I to get along? I had been trying for weeks, in vain, to get a good seamstress; and yet had no prospect of obtaining one. I was going to lose my cook, and, in all probability, my chambermaid. What would I do? No light broke in through the cloudy veil that overhung my mind. The door opened, and Agnes, who had come up to my room, said -

"Mrs. Partridge is done."

I took out my purse, and had selected therefrom the change necessary to pay the washerwoman, when a thought of her caused me to say -

"Tell Mrs. Partridge to come up and see me."

My thoughts and feelings were changing. By the time the washerwoman came in, my interest in her was alive again.

"Sit down," said I, to the tired-looking creature who sank into a chair, evidently much wearied.

"It's hard work, Mrs. Partridge," said I.

"Yes, ma'am, it is rather hard. But I am thankful for health and strength to enable me to go through with it. I know some poor women who have to work as hard as I do, and yet do not know what it is to feel well for an hour at a time."

"Poor creatures!" said I. "It is very hard! How in the world can they do it?"

"We can do a great deal, ma'am, when it comes the pinch; and it is much pleasanter to do, I find, than to think about it. If I were to think much I should give up in despair. But I pray the Lord each morning to give me my daily bread, and thus far he has done it, and will, I am sure, continue to do it to the end."

"Happy it is for you that you can so think and feel," I replied. "But I am sure I could not be as you are, Mrs. Partridge. It would kill me."

"I sincerely trust, ma'am, that you will never be called to pass through what I have," said Mrs. Partridge. "And yet there are those who have it still harder. There

T.S. Arthur

was a time when the thought of being as poor as I now am, and of having to work so hard, would have been terrible to me; and yet I do not know that I was so very much happier then than I am now, though I confess I ought to have been. I had full and plenty of every thing brought into the house by my husband, and had only to dispense in my family the blessings of God sent to us. But I let things annoy me then more than they do now."

"But how can you help being worried, Mrs. Partridge? To be away from my children as you have been away from yours all day would set me wild. I would be sure some of them would be killed or dreadfully hurt."

"Children are wonderfully protected," said Mrs. Partridge, in a confident voice.

"So they are. But to think of four little children, the youngest eleven months and the oldest not ten years old, left all alone, for a whole day!"

"It is bad when we think about it, I know," returned Mrs. Partridge. "It looks very bad! But I try and put that view of it out of my mind. When I leave them in the morning they say they will be good children. At dinner time I sometimes find them all fast asleep or playing about. I never find them crying, or at all unhappy. Jane loves the younger ones, and keeps them pleased all the time. In the evening, when I get back from my work, there is generally no one awake but Jane. She has given them the bread and milk I left for their suppers, and undressed and put them to bed."

"Dear little girl! What a treasure she must be!" I could not help saying.

"She is, indeed. I don't see how I could get along without her."

"You could not get along at all."

"Oh, yes, ma'am, I could. Some way would be provided for me," was the confident reply.

I looked into the poor woman's face with wonder and admiration. So patient, so trustful, and yet so very poor. The expression of her countenance was beautiful in its calm religious hope, and it struck me more than ever as familiar.

"Did I ever see you before, Mrs. Partridge?" I asked.

"Indeed, ma'am, I don't know. I am sure I have seen you somewhere. No, now I recollect; it is your likeness to a young schoolmate that makes your face so familiar. How much you do favour her, now I look at you more closely."

"What was her name?" I asked.

"Her name was Flora S -"

"Indeed! Why, that was my name!"

"Your name! Did you go to Madame Martier's school?"

"I did."

"And can you indeed be my old schoolmate, Flora S -?"

"My maiden name was Flora S -, and I went to

Madame Martier's. Your face is also familiar, but how to place you I do not know."

"Don't you remember Helen Sprague?"

"Helen Sprague! This can't be Helen Sprague, surely! Yes! I remember now. Why, Helen?" and I stepped forward and grasped her hand. "I am both glad and sorry to see you. To think that, after the lapse of fifteen years, we should meet thus! How in the world is it that fortune has been so unkind to you? I remember hearing it said that you had married very well."

"I certainly never had cause to regret my marriage," replied Mrs. Partridge, with more feeling than she had yet shown. "While my husband lived I had every external blessing that I could ask. But, just before he died, somehow or other he got behind-hand in his business, and after his death, there being no one to see to things, what he left was seized upon and sold, leaving me friendless and almost penniless. Since then, the effort to get food and clothes for my children has been so constant and earnest, that I have scarcely had time to sit down and grieve over my losses and sufferings. It is one perpetual struggle for life. And yet, though I cannot now keep the tears from my eyes, I will not say that I am unhappy. Thus far, all things necessary for me have come. I yet have my little flock together, and a place that bears the sacred name of home."

I looked into Helen's face, over which tears were falling, and wondered if I were not dreaming. At school she had been the favourite of all, she was so full of good humour, and had such a cheerful, peace-loving spirit. Her parents were poor, but respectable people, who died when Helen was fifteen years old. She was then taken from school, and I never saw her afterward until she came to my house in the capacity of a washerwoman, hundreds of miles away from the scenes of our early years.

"But can't you find easier work than washing?" I asked. "Are you not handy with your needle?"

"The only work I have been able to get has been from the clothing men, and they pay so little that I can't live on it."

"Can you do fine sewing?" I asked.

"Yes, I call myself handy with my needle."

"Can you make children's clothes?"

"Boy's clothes?"

"No. Girl's clothing."

"Oh, yes."

"I'm very much in want of some one. My children are all in" - rags and tatters I was going to say, but I checked myself - "are all in need of clothes, and so far I have not been able to get anybody to sew for me. If you like, I will give you three or four weeks' sewing at least."

"I shall be very glad to have it, and very thankful for your kindness in offering it to me," returned Mrs. Partridge, rising from her chair, and adding as she did so -

"But I must be getting home. It is nearly dark, and Jane will be anxious to see me back again."

I handed her the seventy-five cents she had earned for washing for me during a whole day. Promising to come over and see me early in the morning about the sewing, she withdrew, and I was left again to my own reflections.

"If ever a murmurer and complainer received a severe rebuke, it is I!" was the first almost audible thought that passed through my mind. "To think that I, with my cup full and running over with blessings, should make myself and all around me unhappy, because a few minor things are not just to my satisfaction, while this woman, who toils like a slave from morning until night, and who can hardly procure food and clothing for her children, from whom she is almost constantly separated, is patient and hopeful, makes me feel as if I deserved to lose what I have refused to enjoy."

On the next morning Mrs. Partridge called quite early. She cut and fitted several frocks for the children, at which work she seemed very handy, and then took them home to make. She sewed for me five weeks, and then got work in another family where I recommended her. Since then, she has been kept constantly employed in sewing, at good prices, by about six families. In all of these I have spoken of her and created an interest in her favour. The mere wages that she earns is much less than what she really receives. All her children's clothes are given to her, and she receives many a bag of meal and load of coal without knowing from whence it comes. In fact, her condition is more comfortable in every way than it was, and, in fact, so is mine. The lesson of patience I learned from Mrs. Partridge in my first, and in many subsequent interviews, impressed itself deeply upon my mind, and caused me to look at and value the good I had, rather than fret over the few occurrences that were not altogether to my wishes. I saw, too, how the small trouble to me had been the means of working out a great good to her. My need of a washerwoman, about which I had been so annoyed, and the temporary want of a seamstress which I had experienced - light things as they should have been - led me to search about for aid, and, providentially, to fall upon Mrs. Partridge, who needed just what it was in my power to do for her.

Whenever I find myself falling into my old habit, which I am sorry to say is too frequently the case, I turn my thoughts to this poor woman, who is still toiling on under heavy life-burdens, yet with meekness and patience, and bowing my head in shame, say -

"If *she* is thankful for the good she has, how deep should be *my* gratitude!"

I DIDN'T THINK OF THAT!

MR. LAWSON, the tailor, was considered a very good member of society. He was industrious, paid what he owed, was a kind husband and father and a pleasant and considerate neighbour. He was, moreover, attached to the church, and, by his brethren in the faith, considered a pious and good man. And, to say the truth, Mr. Lawson would compare favourably with most people.

One day as Mr. Lawson stood at his cutting board, shears in hand, a poorly dressed young woman entered his shop, and approaching him, asked, with some embarrassment and timidity, if he had any work to give out.

"What can you do?" asked the tailor, looking rather coldly upon his visitor.

"I can make pantaloons and vests," replied the girl.

"Have you ever worked for the merchant tailors?"

"Yes, sir, I worked for Mr. Wright."

"Hasn't he any thing for you to do?"

"No, not just now. He has regular hands who always

get the preference."

"Did your work suit him?"

"He never found fault with it."

"Where do you live?"

"In Cherry street," replied the young woman.

"At No. -"

Mr. Lawson stood and mused for a short time.

"I have a vest here," he at length said, taking a small bundle from a shelf, "which I want by tomorrow evening at the latest. If you think you can make it very neatly, and have it done in time, you can take it."

"It shall be done in time," said the young woman, reaching out eagerly for the bundle.

"And remember, I shall expect it made well. If I like your work, I will give you more."

"I will try to please you," returned the girl, in a low voice.

"To-morrow evening, recollect."

"Yes, sir. I will have it done."

The girl turned and went quickly away. As she walked along hurriedly, her slender form bent forward, and there was an unsteadiness in her steps, as if from weakness. She did not linger a moment, nor heed any thing that was passing in the street.

A back room in the third story of an old house in Cherry street was the home of the poor sewing girl. As she entered, she said, in a cheerful voice, to a person who was lying upon a bed which the room contained -

"I have got work, sister. It is a vest, and it must be done by to-morrow evening."

"Can you finish it in time?" inquired the invalid in a faint voice.

"Oh, yes, easily;" and as she spoke, she laid off her bonnet and shawl hurriedly and sat down to unroll the work she had obtained.

The vest proved to be of white Marseilles. As soon as the invalid sister saw this, she said -

"I'm afraid you won't be able to get that done in time, Ellen; it is very particular work. To stitch the edges well will alone take you many hours."

"I will sit up late, and get a fair start to-night, Mary. Then I can easily finish it in time. You know a vest is only a day's work for a good sewer, and I have nearly a day and a half before me."

"Yes; but you must remember, Ellen, that you are not very fast with your needle, and are, besides, far from being well. The work, too, is of the most particular kind, and cannot be hurried."

"Don't fear for me in the least, Mary. I will do all I have engaged to do," and the young woman, who had already arranged the cut-out garment, took a portion of it in her lap and commenced her task.

The two sisters, here introduced, were poor, in bad health, and without friends. Mary, the older, had declined rapidly within a few months, and become so much exhausted as to be obliged to keep her bed most of the time. The task of providing for the wants of both fell, consequently, upon Ellen. Increased exertion was more than her delicate frame could well endure. Daily were the vital energies of her system becoming more and more exhausted, a fact of which she was painfully conscious, and which she, with studious care, sought to conceal from Mary.

When, through loss of friends and change of circumstances, the two sisters were thrown entirely dependent upon their own exertions for a livelihood, they, with prudent forethought, immediately applied themselves to the learning of a trade in order to have the means of support. Confinement for twelve or fourteen hours a day, sitting in one position - a great change for them - could not long be endured without producing ill effects on frail young creatures at best. Mary, the older, failed first; and, at the time of which we are writing, had so far declined as to be little more than the shadow of any thing earthly.

With her own unaided hands, Ellen found it impossible to earn enough for even their most simple need. Often Mary was without medicine, because there was no money left after food and fuel were bought. More and more earnestly did Ellen apply herself as want came in more varied shapes; but the returns of her labour became daily less and less adequate to meet the demands of nature.

T.S. Arthur

The busy season had passed, and trade was dull. Ellen worked for only two merchant tailors, and with them she was considered an extra hand. When business fell off, as the season approached towards mid-summer, she was the first to receive notice that no more work could be given out for the present. With a disheartened feeling she returned home on receiving this intelligence. Mary saw that something was wrong the moment she entered, and tenderly inquired the cause of her trouble. On learning what it was, she endeavoured to comfort and assure her, but to little purpose.

As soon as Ellen could regain sufficient composure of mind, she went forth in search of work at other shops. To one of her peculiar, timid, and shrinking disposition this was a severe trial. But there was no passing it by. Three days elapsed, during which every effort to get work proved unsuccessful. Even the clothing stores had nothing to give out to extra hands.

Reduced to their last penny, Ellen was almost in despair, when she called upon Mr. Lawson. The garment he gave her to make seemed to her like help sent from heaven. Cheerfully did she work upon it until a late hour at night, and she was ready to resume her labour with the rising sun. But, as Mary had feared, the work did not progress altogether to her satisfaction. She had never made over one or two white Marseilles vests, and found that she was not so well skilled in the art of neat and accurate stitching as was required to give the garment a beautiful and workmanlike appearance. The stitches did not impress themselves along the edges with the accuracy that her eye told her was required, and she was troubled to find that, be as careful as she would, the pure white fabric grew soiled beneath her fingers. Mary, to whom she frequently submitted the work, tried to encourage her; but her eyes were not deceived.

It was after dark when Ellen finished the garment. She was weary and faint; for she had taken no food since morning, and had been bending over her work, with very little intermission, the whole day; and she had no hope of receiving any thing more to do, for Mr. Lawson, she was sure, would not be pleased with the way the vest was made. But, want of every thing, and particularly food for herself and sister, made the sum of seventy-five cents, to be received for the garment, a little treasure in her eyes; and she hurried off with the vest the moment it was finished.

"I will bring home a little tea, sister," she said, as she was about leaving; "I am sure a cup of tea will do you good; and I feel as if it would revive and strengthen me."

Mary looked at Ellen with a tender, pitying expression, while her large bright eyes shone glassy in the dim rays sent forth by a poor lamp; but she did not reply. She had a gnawing in her stomach, that made her feel faint, and a most earnest craving for nourishing and even stimulating food, the consequence of long abstinence as well as from the peculiarity of her disease. But she did not breathe a word of this to Ellen, who would, she knew, expend for her every cent of the money she was about to receive, if she was aware of the morbid appetite from which she was suffering.

"I will be back soon," added Ellen, as she retired from the room.

Mary sighed deeply when alone. She raised her eyes

T.S. Arthur

upwards for a few moments, then closing them and clasping her hands tightly together, she lay with her white face turned towards the light, more the image of death than of life.

"Here it is past eight o'clock, and that vest is not yet in," said Mr. Lawson, in a fretful tone. "I had my doubts about the girl when I gave it to her. But she looked so poor, and seemed so earnest about work, that I was weak enough to intrust her with the garment. But I will take care, another time, how I let my feeling get the better of my judgment."

Before the individual had time to reply, Ellen came in with the vest, and laid it on the counter, at which the tailor was standing. She said nothing, neither did the tailor make any remark; but the latter unfolded the vest in the way that plainly showed him not to be in a very placid frame of mind.

"Goodness!" he ejaculated, after glancing hurriedly at the garment.

The girl shrunk back from the counter, and looked frightened.

"Well, this is a pretty job for one to bring in!" said the tailor, in an excited tone of voice. "A pretty job, indeed! It looks as if it had been dragged through a duck puddle. And such work!"

He tossed the garment from him in angry contempt, and walked away to the back part of the shop, leaving Ellen standing almost as still as a statue.

"That vest was to have been home to-night," he said, as

he threw himself into a chair. "Of course, the customer will be disappointed and angry, and I shall lose him. But I don't care half so much for that, as I do for not being able to keep my word with him. It is too much!"

Ellen would have instantly retired, but the thought of her sick sister forced her to remain. She felt that she could not go until she had received the price of making the vest, for their money was all gone, and they had no food in the house. She had lingered for a little while, when the tailor called out to her, and said -

"You needn't stand there, Miss! thinking that I am going to pay you for ruining the job. It's bad enough to lose my material, and customer into the bargain. In justice you should be made to pay for the vest. But there is no hope for that. So take yourself away as quickly as possible, and never let me set eyes on you again."

Ellen did not reply, but turned away slowly, and, with her eyes upon the floor and her form drooping, retired from the shop. After she had gone, Mr. Lawson returned to the front part of the store, and taking up the vest, brought it back to where an elderly man was sitting, and holding it towards him, said, by way of apology for the part he had taken in the little scene:

"That's a beautiful article for a gentleman to wear - isn't it?"

The man made no reply, and the tailor, after a pause, added -

"I refused to pay her, as a matter of principle. She knew she couldn't make the garment when she took it

T.S. Arthur

away. She will be more careful how she tries again to impose herself upon customer tailors as a good vest maker."

"Perhaps," said the old gentleman, in a mild way, "necessity drove her to you for work, and tempted her to undertake a job that required greater skill than she possessed. She certainly looked very poor."

"It was because she appeared so poor and miserable that I was weak enough to place the vest in her hands," replied Mr. Lawson, in a less severe tone of voice. "But it was an imposition in her to ask for work that she did not know how to make."

"Brother Lawson," said the old gentleman, who was a fellow member of the church, "we should not blame, with too much severity, the person who, in extreme want, undertakes to perform work for which he does not possess the requisite skill. The fact that a young girl, like the one who was just here, is willing, in her extreme poverty, to labour, instead of sinking into vice and idleness, shows her to possess both virtue and integrity of character, and these we should be willing to encourage, even at some sacrifice. Work is slack now, as you are aware, and there is but little doubt that she had been to many places seeking employment before she came to you. It may be - and this is a very probable suggestion - that she did not come to you for work until she, and those who may be dependent upon the meagre returns of her labour, were reduced to the utmost extremity. And, it may be, that even their next meal was dependent upon the receipt of the money that was expected to be paid for making the vest you hold in your hand. The expression of her face as she turned away, and her slow, lingering step and drooping form, as she left the shop, had in them a language which told me of all this, and even more."

A great change came over the tailor's countenance.

"I didn't think of that," fell in a low tone from his lips.

"I didn't suppose you did, brother Lawson," said his monitor. "We are all more apt to think of ourselves than of others. The girl promised you the vest this evening?"

"Yes."

"And, so far as that was concerned, performed her contract. Is the vest made so very badly?"

Mr. Lawson took up the garment, and examined it more carefully.

"Well, I can't say that the work is so very badly done. But it is dreadfully soiled and rumpled, and is not as neat a job as it should be, nor at all such as I wished it. The customer for whom it is intended is very particular, and I was anxious to please him."

"All this is very annoying, of course; but still we should always be ready to make some excuse for the short-comings of others. There is no telling under how many disadvantages the poor girl may have laboured in making this vest. She may have had a sick mother, or a father, or sister to attend to, which constantly interfered with and interrupted her. She may have been compelled, from this cause, to work through a greater part of the night, in order to keep her promise to you. Under such circumstances, even you could hardly wonder if the garment were not made well, or if it came soiled from her hands. And even you could hardly find it in your heart to speak unkindly to the poor creature, much less turn her away angrily, and without the money she had toiled for so earnestly."

"I didn't think of that," was murmured in a low abstracted voice.

"Who could wonder," continued the old man, "if that unhappy girl, deprived of the reward of honest labour, and driven angrily away as you drove her just now, should in despair step aside into ruin, thus sacrificing herself, body and soul, in order to save from want and deprivation those she could not sustain by virtuous toil?"

"I didn't think of that," fell quick and in an agitated voice from the tailor's lips, as, dropping the garment he held in his hand, he hurried around his counter and left the shop.

Ellen was not tempted as the friend of Mr. Lawson had supposed; but there are hundreds who, under like circumstances, would have turned aside. From the shop of the tailor she went slowly homeward; at her heart was a feeling of utter despondency. She had struggled long, in weariness and pain, with her lot; but now she felt that the struggle was over. The hope of the hour had failed, and it seemed to her the last hope.

When Ellen entered the room where her sister lay, the sight of her expectant face (for the desire for nourishing, refreshing food had been stronger than usual with Mary, and her fancy had been dwelling upon the pleasant repast that was soon to be spread before her) made the task of communicating the cruel repulse she had received tenfold more painful. Without uttering a word, she threw herself upon the bed beside her sister, and, burying her face in a pillow, endeavoured to smother the sobs that came up convulsively from her bosom. Mary asked no question. She understood the meaning of Ellen's agitation well; it told her that she had been disappointed in the expectation of receiving the money for her work.

Deep silence followed. Mary clasped her hands together and raised her eyes upward, while Ellen lay motionless with her face hidden where she had first concealed it. There was a knock at the door, but no voice bade the applicant for admission enter. It was repeated; but, if heard, it met no response. Then the latch was lifted, the door swung open, and the tailor stepped into the room. The sound of his feet aroused the passive sisters. The white face of Mary was to him, at first, a startling image of death; but her large bright eyes opened and turned upon him with an assurance that life still lingered in its earthly tenement.

"Ellen, Ellen," said the sick girl, faintly.

Ellen, too, had heard the sound of footsteps on the floor, and she now raised up slowly, and presented to Lawson her sad, tearful countenance.

"I was wrong to speak to you as I did," said the tailor without preface, advancing towards the bed and holding out to Ellen the money she had earned. "There is the price of the vest; it is better made than I at first thought it was. To-morrow I will send you more work. Try and cheer up. Are you so very poor?"

The last two sentences were uttered in a voice of encouragement and sympathy. Ellen looked her thankfulness, but did not venture a reply. Her heart was too full to trust her lips with utterance.

Feeling that his presence, under all circumstances, could not but be embarrassing, Mr. Lawson, after taking two or three dollars from his pocket and placing them on the table with the remark - "Take this in advance for work," retired and left the poor sisters in a different frame of mind from what they were in when he entered. Shortly after they received a basket, in which was a supply of nourishing food. Though no one's name was sent with it, they were not in doubt as to whence it came.

Mr. Lawson was not an unfeeling man, but, like too many others in the world, he did not always "think."

TAKING BOARDERS

CHAPTER I

A LADY, past the prime of life, sat thoughtful, as twilight fell duskily around her, in a room furnished with great elegance. That her thoughts were far from being pleasant, the sober, even sad expression of her countenance too clearly testified. She was dressed in deep mourning. A faint sigh parted her lips as she looked up, on hearing the door of the apartment in which she was sitting open. The person who entered, a tall and beautiful girl, also in mourning, came and sat down by her side, and leaned her head, with a pensive, troubled air, down upon her shoulder.

"We must decide upon something, Edith, and that with as little delay as possible," said the elder of the two ladies, soon after the younger one entered. This was said in a tone of great despondency.

"Upon what shall we decide, mother?" and the young lady raised her head from its reclining position, and looked earnestly into the eyes of her parent.

"We must decide to do something by which the family can be sustained. Your father's death has left us, unfortunately and unexpectedly, as you already know, with scarcely a thousand dollars beyond the furniture of this house, instead of an independence which we supposed him to possess. His death was sad and afflictive enough - more than it seemed I could bear. But to have this added!"

The voice of the speaker sank into a low moan, and was lost in a stifled sob.

"But what *can* we do, mother?" asked Edith, in an earnest tone, after pausing long enough for her mother to regain the control of her feelings.

"I have thought of but one thing that is at all respectable," replied the mother.

"What is that?"

"Taking boarders."

"Why, mother!" ejaculated Edith, evincing great surprise, "how can you think of such a thing?"

"Because driven to do so by the force of circum-stances."

"Taking boarders! Keeping a boarding-house! Surely we have not come to this!"

An expression of distress blended with the look of astonishment in Edith's face.

"There is nothing disgraceful in keeping a boarding-house," returned the mother. "A great many very respectable ladies have been compelled to resort to it as a means of supporting their families."

"But to think of it, mother! To think of *your* keeping a boarding-house! I cannot bear it."

"Is there any thing else that can be done, Edith?"

"Don't ask *me* such a question."

"If, then, you cannot think for me, you must try and think with me, my child. Something will have to be done to create an income. In less than twelve months, every dollar I have will be expended; and then what are we to do? Now, Edith, is the time for us to look at the matter earnestly, and to determine the course we will take. There is no use to look away from it. A good house in a central situation, large enough for the purpose, can no doubt be obtained; and I think there will be no difficulty about our getting boarders enough to fill it. The income or profit from these will enable us still to live comfortably, and keep Edward and Ellen at school."

"It is hard," was the only remark Edith made to this.

"It is hard, my daughter; very hard! I have thought and thought about it until my whole mind has been thrown into confusion. But it will not do to think for ever; there must be action. Can I see want stealing in upon my children, and sit and fold my hands supinely? No! And to you, Edith, my oldest child, I look for aid and for counsel. Stand up bravely by my side."

"And you are in earnest in all this?" said Edith, whose mind seemed hardly able to realize the truth of their position. From her earliest days, all the blessings that money could procure had been freely scattered around her feet. As she grew up and advanced towards womanhood, she had moved in the most fashionable circles, and there acquired the habit of estimating people according to their wealth and social standing, rather than by qualities of mind. In her view, it appeared degrading in a woman to enter upon any kind of employment for money; and with the keeper of a boarding-house, particularly, she had always associated something low, vulgar, and ungenteel. At the thought of her mother's engaging in such an occupation, when the suggestion was made her mind instantly revolted. It appeared to her as if disgrace would be the inevitable consequence.

"And you are in earnest in all this?" was an expression mingling her clear conviction of the truth of what at first appeared so strange a proposition, and her astonishment that the necessities of their situation were such as to drive them to so humiliating a resource.

"Deeply in earnest," was the mother's reply.

"We are left alone in the world. He who cared for us and provided for us so liberally has been taken away, and we have nowhere to look for aid but to the resources that are in ourselves. These well applied, will give us, I feel strongly assured, all that we need. The thing to decide is, what we ought to do. If we choose aright, all will doubtless come out right. To choose aright is, therefore, of the first importance; and to do this, we must not suffer distorting suggestions nor the appeals of a false pride to influence our minds in the least. You are my oldest child, Edith; and, as such, I cannot but look upon you as, to some extent, jointly with me, the guardian of your younger brothers and sisters. True, Miriam is of age, and Henry nearly so; but still you are the eldest - your mind is more matured, and in your judgment I have the most confidence. Try and forget, Edith, all but the fact that, unless we make an exertion, one home for all cannot be retained. Are you willing that we should be scattered like leaves in the autumn wind? No! you would consider that one of the greatest calamities that could befall us - an evil to prevent which we should use every effort in our power. Do you, not see this clearly?"

"I do, mother," was replied by Edith in a more rational tone of voice than that in which she had yet spoken.

"To open a store of any kind would involve five times the exposure of a boarding-house; and, moreover, I know nothing of business."

"Keeping a store? Oh, no! we couldn't do that. Think of the dreadful exposure!"

"But in taking boarders we only increase our family, and all goes on as usual. To my mind, it is the most genteel thing that we can do. Our style of living will be the same; our waiter and all our servants will be retained. In fact, to the eye there will be little change, and the world need never know how greatly reduced our circumstances have become."

This mode of argument tended to reconcile Edith to taking boarders. Something, she saw, had to be done. Opening a store was felt to be out of the question; and as to commencing a school, the thought was repulsed at the very first suggestion.

A few friends were consulted on the subject, and all agreed that the best thing for the widow to do was to take boarders. Each one could point to some lady who had commenced the business with far less ability to make boarders comfortable, and who had yet got along very well. It was conceded on all hands that it was a very genteel business, and that some of the first ladies had been compelled to resort to it, without being any the less respected. Almost every one to whom the matter was referred spoke in favour of the thing, and but a single individual suggested difficulty; but what he said was not permitted to have much weight. This individual was a brother of the widow, who had always been looked upon as rather eccentric. He was a bachelor and without fortune, merely enjoying a moderate income as book-keeper in the office of an insurance company. But more of him hereafter.

CHAPTER II

MRS. DARLINGTON, the widow we have just introduced to the reader, had five children. Edith, the oldest daughter, was twenty-two years of age at the time of her father's death; and Henry, the oldest son, just twenty. Next to Henry was Miriam, eighteen years old. The ages of the two youngest children, Ellen and Edward, were ten and eight.

Mr. Darlington, while living, was a lawyer of distinguished ability, and his talents and reputation at the Philadelphia bar enabled him to accumulate a handsome fortune. Upon this he had lived for some years in a style of great elegance. About a year before his death, he had been induced to enter into some speculation that promised great results; but he found, when too late to retreat, that he had been greatly deceived. Heavy losses soon followed. In a struggle to recover himself, he became still further involved; and, ere the expiration of a twelvemonth, saw every thing falling from under him. The trouble brought on by this was the real cause of his death, which was sudden, and resulted from inflammation and congestion of the brain.

Henry Darlington, the oldest son, was a young man of promising talents. He remained at college until a few months before his father's death, when he returned home and commenced the study of law, in which he felt ambitious to distinguish himself.

Edith, the oldest daughter, possessed a fine mind, which had been well educated. She had some false views of life, natural to her position; but, apart from

T.S. Arthur

this, was a girl of sound sense and great force of character. Thus far in life she had not encountered circumstances of a nature calculated to develop what was in her. The time for that, however, was approaching. Miriam, her sister, was a quiet, gentle, retiring, almost timid girl. She went into company with reluctance, and then always shrunk as far from observation as it was possible to get; but, like most quiet, retiring persons, there were deep places in her mind and heart. She thought and felt more than was supposed. All who knew Miriam loved her. Of the younger children we need not here speak.

Mrs. Darlington knew comparatively nothing of the world beyond her own social circle. She was, perhaps, as little calculated for doing what she proposed to do as a woman could well be. She had no habits of economy, and had. never in her life been called upon to make calculations of expense in household matters. There was a tendency to generosity rather than selfishness in her character, and she rarely thought evil of any one. But all that she was need not here be set forth, for it will appear as our narrative progresses.

Mr. Hiram Ellis, the brother of Mrs. Darlington to whom brief allusion has been made, was not a great favourite in the family - although Mr. Darlington understood his good qualities, and very highly respected him - because he had not much that was prepossessing in his external appearance, and was thought to be a little eccentric. Moreover, he was not rich - merely holding the place of book-keeper in an insurance office, at a moderate salary. But as he had never married, and had only himself to support, his income supplied amply all his wants, and left him a small annual surplus.

After the death of Mr. Darlington, he visited his sister much more frequently than before. Of the exact condition of her affairs, he was much better acquainted than she supposed. The anxiety which she felt, some months after her husband's death, when the result of the settlement of his estate became known, led her to be rather more communicative. After determining to open a boarding-house, she said to him, on the occasion of his visiting her one evening -

"As it is necessary for me to do something, Hiram, I have concluded to move to a better location, and take a few boarders."

"Don't do any such thing, Margaret," her brother made answer. "Taking boarders! It's the last thing of which a woman should think."

"Why do you say that, Hiram?" asked Mrs. Darlington, evincing no little surprise at this unexpected reply.

"Because I think that a woman who has a living to make can hardly try a more doubtful experiment. Not one in ten ever succeeds in doing any thing."

"But why, Hiram? Why? I'm sure a great many ladies get a living in that way."

"What you will never do, Margaret, mark my words for it. It takes a woman of shrewdness, caution, and knowledge of the world, and one thoroughly versed in household economy, to get along in this pursuit. Even if you possessed all these prerequisites to success, you have just the family that ought not to come in contact with anybody and everybody that find their way into boarding-houses."

T.S. Arthur

"I must do something, Hiram," said Mrs. Darlington, evincing impatience at the opposition of her brother.

"I perfectly agree with you in that, Margaret," replied Mr. Ellis. "The only doubt is as to your choice of occupation. You think that your best plan will be to take boarders; while I think you could not fall upon a worse expedient."

"Why do you think so?"

"Have I not just said?"

"What?"

"Why, that, in the first place, it takes a woman of great shrewdness, caution, and knowledge of the world, and one thoroughly versed in household economy, to succeed in the business."

"I'm not a fool, Hiram!" exclaimed Mrs. Darlington, losing her self-command.

"Perhaps you may alter your opinion on that head some time within the next twelve months," coolly returned Mr. Ellis, rising and beginning to button up his coat.

"Such language to me, at this time, is cruel!" said Mrs. Darlington, putting her handkerchief to her eyes.

"No," calmly replied her brother, "not cruel, but kind. I wish to save you from trouble."

"What else can I do?" asked the widow, removing the handkerchief from her face.

"Many things, I was going to say," returned Mr. Ellis. "But, in truth, the choice of employment is not very great. Still, something with a fairer promise than taking boarders may be found."

"If you can point me to some better way, brother," said Mrs. Darlington, "I shall feel greatly indebted to you."

"Almost any thing is better. Suppose you and Edith were to open a school. Both of you are well -"

"Open a school!" exclaimed Mrs. Darlington, interrupting her brother, and exhibiting most profound astonishment. "*I* open a school! I didn't think *you* would take advantage of my grief and misfortune to offer me an insult."

Mr. Ellis buttoned the top button of his coat nervously, as his sister said this, and, partly turning himself towards the door, said -

"Teaching school is a far more useful, and, if you will, more respectable employment, than keeping a boarding-house. This you ought to see at a glance. As a teacher, you would be a minister of truth to the mind, and have it in your power to bend from evil and lead to good the young immortals committed to your care; while, as a boarding-house keeper, you would merely furnish food for the natural body - a use below what you are capable of rendering to society."

But Mrs. Darlington was in no state of mind to feel the force of such an argument. From the thought of a school she shrunk as from something degrading, and turned from it with displeasure.

T.S. Arthur

"Don't mention such a thing to me," said she fretfully, "I will not listen to the proposition."

"Oh, well, Margaret, as you please," replied her brother, now moving towards the door. "When you ask my advice, I will give it according to my best judgment, and with a sincere desire for your good. If, however, it conflicts with your views, reject it; but, in simple justice to me, do so in a better spirit than you manifest on the present occasion. Good evening!"

Mrs. Darlington was too much disturbed in mind to make a reply, and Mr. Hiram Ellis left the room without any attempt on the part of his sister to detain him. On both sides there had been the indulgence of rather more impatience and intolerance than was commendable.

CHAPTER III

IN due time, Mrs. Darlington removed to a house in Arch Street, the annual rent of which was six hundred dollars, and there began her experiment. The expense of a removal, and the cost of the additional chamber furniture required, exhausted about two hundred dollars of the widow's slender stock of money, and caused her, to feel a little troubled when she noticed the diminution.

She began her new business with two boarders, a gentleman and his wife by the name of Grimes, who had entered her house on the recommendation of a friend. They were to pay her the sum of eight dollars a week. A young man named Barling, clerk in a wholesale Market Street house, came next; and he introduced, soon after, a friend of his, a clerk in the same store, named Mason. They were room-mates, and paid three dollars and a half each. Three or four weeks elapsed before any further additions were made; then an advertisement brought several applications. One was from a gentleman who wanted two rooms for himself and wife, a nurse and four children. He wanted the second story front and back chambers, furnished, and was not willing to pay over sixteen dollars, although his oldest child was twelve and his youngest four years of age - seven good eaters and two of the best rooms in the house for sixteen dollars!

Mrs. Darlington demurred. The man said -

"Very well, ma'am," in a tone of indifference. "I can find plenty of accommodations quite as good as yours for the price I offer. It's all I pay now." Poor Mrs.

T.S. Arthur

Darlington sighed. She had but fifteen dollars yet in the house - that is, boarders who paid this amount weekly - and the rent alone amounted to twelve dollars. Sixteen dollars, she argued with herself, as she sat with her eyes upon the floor, would make a great difference in her income; would, in fact, meet all the expenses of the house. Two good rooms would still remain, and all that she received for these would be so much clear profit. Such was the hurried conclusion of Mrs. Darlington's mind.

"I suppose I will have to take you," said she, lifting her eyes to the man's hard features. "But those rooms ought to bring me twenty-four dollars."

"Sixteen is the utmost I will pay," replied the man. In fact, I did think of offering only fourteen dollars. "But the rooms are fine, and I like them. Sixteen is a liberal price. Your terms are considerably above the ordinary range."

The widow sighed again.

If the man heard this sound, it did not touch a single chord of feeling.

"Then it is understood that I am to have your rooms at sixteen dollars?" said he.

"Yes, sir. I will take you for that."

"Very well. My name is Scragg. We will be ready to come in on Monday next. You can have all prepared for us?"

"Yes, sir."

Scarcely had Mr. Scragg departed, when a gentleman called to know if Mrs. Darlington had a vacant front room in the second story.

"I had this morning; but it is taken," replied the widow.

"Ah! I'm sorry for that."

"Will not a third story front room suit you?" "No. My wife is not in very good health, and wishes a second story room. We pay twelve dollars a week, and would even give more, if necessary, to obtain just the accommodations we like. The situation of your house pleases me. I'm sorry that I happen to be too late."

"Will you look at the room?" said Mrs. Darlington, into whose mind came the desire to break the bad bargain she had just made.

"If you please," returned the man.

And both went up to the large and beautifully furnished chambers.

"Just the thing!" said the man, as he looked around, much pleased with the appearance of every thing. "But I understood you to say that it was taken."

"Why, yes," replied Mrs. Darlington, "I did partly engage it this morning; but, no doubt, I can arrange with the family to take the two rooms above, which will suit them just as well."

"If you can" -

"There'll be no difficulty, I presume. You'll pay twelve

T.S. Arthur

dollars a week?"

"Yes."

"Only yourself and lady?"

"That's all."

"Very well, sir; you can have the room."

"It's a bargain, then. My name is Ring. Our week is up to-day where we are; and, if it is agreeable, we will become your guests to-morrow."

"Perfectly agreeable, Mr. Ring."

The gentleman bowed politely and retired.

Now Mrs. Darlington did not feel very comfortable when she reflected on what she had done. The rooms in the second story were positively engaged to Mr. Scragg, and now one of them was as positively engaged to Mr. Ring. The face of Mr. Scragg she remembered very well. It was a hard, sinister face, just such a one as we rarely forget because of the disagreeable impression it makes. As it came up distinctly before the eyes of her mind, she was oppressed with a sense of coming trouble. Nor did she feel altogether satisfied with what she had done - satisfied in her own conscience.

On the next morning, Mr. and Mrs. Ring came and took possession of the room previously engaged to Mr. Scragg. They were pleasant people, and made a good first impression.

As day after day glided past, Mrs. Darlington felt more and more uneasy about Mr. Scragg, with whom, she had a decided presentiment, there would be trouble. Had she known where to find him, she would have sent him a note, saying that she had changed her mind about the rooms, and could not let him have them. But she was ignorant of his address; and the only thing left for her was to wait until he came on Monday, and then get over the difficulty in the best way possible. She and Edith had talked over the matter frequently, and had come to the determination to offer Mr. Scragg the two chambers in the third story for fourteen dollars.

On Monday morning, Mrs. Darlington was nervous. This was the day on which Mr. Scragg and family were to arrive, and she felt that there would be trouble.

Mr. Ring, and the other gentlemen boarders, left soon after breakfast. About ten o'clock, the door-bell rang. Mrs. Darlington was in her room at the time changing her dress. Thinking that this might be the announcement of Mr. Scragg's arrival, she hurried through her dressing in order to get down to the parlour as quickly as possible to meet him and the difficulty that was to be encountered; but before she was in a condition to be seen, she heard a man's voice on the stairs, saying -

"Walk up, my dear. The rooms on the second floor are ours."

Then came the noise of many feet in the passage, and the din of children's voices. Mr. Scragg and his family had arrived.

Mrs. Ring was sitting with the morning paper in her hand, when her door was flung widely open, and a

T.S. Arthur

strange man stepped boldly in, saying, as he did so, to the lady who followed him -

"This is one of the chambers."

Mrs. Ring arose, bowed, and looked at the intruders with surprise and embarrassment. Just then, four rude children bounded into the room, spreading themselves around it, and making themselves perfectly at home.

"There is some mistake, I presume," said Mrs. Scragg, on perceiving a lady in the room, whose manner said plainly enough that they were out of their place.

"Oh no! no mistake at all," replied Scragg.

"These are the two rooms I engaged."

Just then Mrs. Darlington entered, in manifest excitement.

"Walk down into the parlour, if you please," said she.

"These are our rooms," said Scragg, showing no inclination to vacate the premises.

"Be kind enough to walk down into the parlour," repeated Mrs. Darlington, whose sense of propriety was outraged by the man's conduct, and who felt a corresponding degree of indignation.

With some show of reluctance, this invitation was acceded to, and Mr. Scragg went muttering down stairs, followed by his brood. The moment he left the chamber, the door was shut and locked by Mrs. Ring, who was a good deal frightened by so unexpected an intrusion.

"What am I to understand by this, madam?" said Mr. Scragg, fiercely, as soon as they had all reached the parlour, planting his hands upon his hips as he spoke, drawing himself up, and looking at Mrs. Darlington with a lowering countenance.

"Take a seat, madam," said Mrs. Darlington, addressing the man's wife in a tone of forced composure. She was struggling for self-possession.

The lady sat down.

"Will you be good enough to explain the meaning of all this, madam?" repeated Mr. Scragg.

"The meaning is simply," replied Mrs. Darlington, "that I have let the front room in the second story to a gentleman and his wife for twelve dollars a week."

"The deuse you have!" said Mr. Scragg, with a particular exhibition of gentlemanly indignation.

"And pray, madam, didn't you let both the rooms in the second story to me for sixteen dollars?"

"I did; but" -

"Oh, very well. That's all I wish to know about it. The rooms were rented to me, and from that day became mine. Please to inform the lady and her husband that I am here with my family, and desire them to vacate the chambers as quickly as possible. I'm a man that knows his rights, and, knowing, always maintains them."

"You cannot have the rooms, sir. That is out of the question," said Mrs. Darlington, looking both distressed and indignant.

"And I tell you that I will have them!" replied Scragg, angrily.

"Peter! Peter! Don't act so," now interposed Mrs. Scragg. "There's no use in it."

"Ain't there, indeed? We'll see. Madam" - he addressed Mrs. Darlington - "will you be kind enough to inform the lady and gentleman who now occupy one of our rooms" -

"Mr. Scragg!" said Mrs. Darlington, in whose fainting heart his outrageous conduct had awakened something of the right spirit - "Mr. Scragg, I wish you to understand, once for all, that the front room is taken and now occupied, and that you cannot have it."

"Madam!"

"It's no use for you to waste words, sir! What I say I mean. I have other rooms in the house very nearly as good, and am willing to take you for something less in consideration of this disappointment. If that will meet your views, well; if not, let us have no more words on the subject."

There was a certain something in Mrs. Darlington's tone of voice that Scragg understood to mean a fixed purpose. Moreover, his mind caught at the idea of getting boarded for something less than sixteen dollars a week.

"Where are the rooms?" he asked gruffly.

"The third story chambers."

"Front?"

"Yes."

"I don't want to go to the third story."

"Very well. Then you can have the back chamber down stairs, and the front chamber above."

"What will be your charge?"

"Fourteen dollars."

"That will do, Peter," said Mrs. Scragg. "Two dollars a week is considerable abatement."

"It's something, of course. But I don't like this off and on kind of business. When I make an agreement, I'm up to the mark, and expect the same from everybody else. Will you let my wife see the rooms, madam?"

"Certainly," replied Mrs. Darlington, and moved towards the door. Mrs. Scragg followed, and so did all the juvenile Scraggs - the latter springing up the stairs with the agility of apes and the noise of a dozen rude schoolboys just freed from the terror of rod and ferule.

The rooms suited Mrs. Scragg very well - at least such was her report to her husband - and, after some further rudeness on the part of Mr. Scragg, and an effort to beat Mrs. Darlington down to twelve dollars a week, were taken, and forthwith occupied.

CHAPTER IV

MRS. DARLINGTON was a woman of refinement herself, and had been used to the society of refined persons. She was, naturally enough, shocked at the coarseness and brutality of Mr. Scragg, and, ere an hour went by, in despair at the unmannerly rudeness of the children, the oldest a stout, vulgar-looking boy, who went racing and rummaging about the house from the garret to the cellar. For a long time after her exciting interview with Mr. Scragg, she sat weeping and trembling in her own room, with Edith by her side, who sought earnestly to comfort and encourage her.

"Oh, Edith!" she sobbed, "to think that we should be humbled to this!"

"Necessity has forced us into our present unhappy position, mother," replied Edith. "Let us meet its difficulties with as brave hearts as possible."

"I shall never be able to treat that dreadful man with even common civility," said Mrs. Darlington.

"We have accepted him as our guest, mother, and it will be our duty to make all as pleasant and comfortable as possible. We will have to bear much, I see - much beyond what I had anticipated."

Mrs. Darlington sighed deeply as she replied -

"Yes, yes, Edith. Ah, the thought makes me miserable!"

"No more of that sweet drawing together in our own

dear home circle," remarked Edith, sadly.

"Henceforth we are to bear the constant presence and intrusion of strangers, with whom we have few or no sentiments in common. We open our house and take in the ignorant, the selfish, the vulgar, and feed them for a certain price! Does not the thought bring a feeling of painful humiliation? What can pay for all this? Ah me! The anticipation had in it not a glimpse of what we have found in our brief experience. Except Mr. and Mrs. Ring, there isn't a lady nor gentleman in the house. That Mason is so rudely familiar that I cannot bear to come near him. He's making himself quite intimate with Henry already, and I don't like to see it."

"Nor do I," replied Mrs. Darlington. "Henry's been out with him twice to the theatre already."

"I'm afraid of his influence over Henry. He's not the kind of a companion he ought to choose," said Edith. "And then Mr. Barling is with Miriam in the parlour almost every evening. He asks her to sing, and she says she doesn't like to refuse."

The mother sighed deeply. While they were conversing, a servant came to their room to say that Mr. Ring was in the parlour, and wished to speak with Mrs. Darlington. It was late in the afternoon of the day on which the Scraggs had made their appearance.

With a presentiment of trouble, Mrs. Darlington went down to the parlour.

"Madam," said Mr. Ring, as soon as she entered, speaking in a firm voice, "I find that my wife has been grossly insulted by a fellow whose family you have

T.S. Arthur

taken into your house. Now they must leave here, or we will, and that forthwith."

"I regret extremely," replied Mrs. Darlington, "the unpleasant occurrence to which you allude; but I do not see how it is possible for me to turn these people out of the house."

"Very well, ma'am. Suit yourself about that. You can choose between us. Both can't remain."

"If I were to tell this Mr. Scragg to seek another boarding-house, he would insult me," said Mrs. Darlington.

"Strange that you would take such a fellow into your house!"

"My rooms were vacant, and I had to fill them."

"Better to have let them remain vacant. But this is neither here nor there. If this fellow remains, we go."

And go they did on the next day. Mrs. Darlington was afraid to approach Mr. Scragg on the subject. Had she done so, she would have received nothing but abuse.

Two weeks afterward, the room vacated by Mr. and Mrs. Ring was taken by a tall, fine-looking man, who wore a pair of handsome whiskers and dressed elegantly. He gave his name as Burton, and agreed to pay eight dollars. Mrs. Darlington liked him very much. There was a certain style about him that evidenced good breeding and a knowledge of the world. What his business was he did not say. He was usually in the house as late as ten o'clock in the morning, and rarely came in before twelve at night.

Soon after Mr. Burton became a member of Mrs. Darlington's household, he began to show particular attentions to Miriam, who was in her nineteenth year, and was, as we have said, a gentle, timid, shrinking girl. Though she did not encourage, she would not reject the attentions of the polite and elegant stranger, who had so much that was agreeable to say that she insensibly acquired a kind of prepossession in his favour.

As now constituted, the family of Mrs. Darlington was not so pleasant and harmonious as could have been desired. Mr. Scragg had already succeeded in making himself so disagreeable to the other boarders, that they were scarcely civil to him; and Mrs. Grimes, who was quite gracious with Mrs. Scragg at first, no longer spoke to her. They had fallen out about some trifle, quarrelled, and then cut each other's acquaintance. When the breakfast, dinner, or tea bell rang, and the boarders assembled at the table, there was generally, at first, an embarrassing silence. Scragg looked like a bull-dog waiting for an occasion to bark; Mrs. Scragg sat with her lips closely compressed and her head partly turned away, so as to keep her eyes out of the line of vision with Mrs. Grimes's face; while Mrs. Grimes gave an occasional glance of contempt towards the lady with whom she had had a "tiff." Barling and Mason, observing all this, and enjoying it, were generally the first to break the reigning silence; and this was usually done by addressing some remark to Scragg, for no other reason, it seemed, than to hear his growling reply. Usually, they succeeded in drawing him into an argument, when they would goad him until he became angry; a species of irritation in which they

T.S. Arthur

never suffered themselves to indulge. As for Mr. Grimes, he was a man of few words. When spoken to, he would reply; but he never made conversation. The only man who really behaved like a gentleman was Mr. Burton; and the contrast seen in him naturally prepossessed the family in his favour.

The first three months' experience in taking boarders was enough to make the heart of Mrs. Darlington sick. All domestic comfort was gone. From early morning until late at night, she toiled harder than any servant in the house; and, with all, had a mind pressed down with care and anxiety. Three times during this period she had been obliged to change her cook, yet, for all, scarcely a day passed that she did not set badly cooked food before her guests. Sometimes certain of the boarders complained, and it generally happened that rudeness accompanied the complaint. The sense of pain that attended this was always most acute, for it was accompanied by deep humiliation and a feeling of helplessness. Moreover, during these first three months, Mr. and Mrs. Grimes had left the house without paying their board for five weeks, thus throwing her into a loss of forty dollars.

At the beginning of this experiment, after completing the furniture of her house, Mrs. Darlington had about three hundred dollars. When the quarter's bill for rent was paid, she had only a hundred and fifty dollars left. Thus, instead of making any thing by boarders, so far, she had sunk a hundred and fifty dollars. This fact disheartened her dreadfully. Then, the effect upon almost every member of her family had been bad. Harry was no longer the thoughtful affectionate, innocent-minded young man of former days. Mason and Barling had introduced him into gay company, and, fascinated with a new and more exciting kind of life, he was fast forming associations and acquiring habits of a dangerous character. It was rare that he spent an evening at home; and, instead of being of any assistance to his mother, was constantly making demands on her for money. The pain all this occasioned Mrs. Darlington was of the most distressing character. Since the children of Mr. and Mrs. Scragg came into the house, Edward and Ellen, who had heretofore been under the constant care and instruction of their mother, left almost entirely to themselves, associated constantly with these children, and learned from them to be rude, vulgar, and, in some things, even vicious. And Miriam had become apparently so much interested in Mr. Burton, who was constantly attentive to her, that both Mrs. Darlington and Edith became anxious on her account. Burton was entire stranger to them all, and there were many things about him that appeared strange, if not wrong.

So much for the experiment of taking boarders, after the lapse of a single quarter of a year.

CHAPTER V

ABOUT this time a lady and gentleman, named Marion, called and engaged boarding for themselves and three children. In Mrs. Marion there was something that won the heart at first sight, and her children were as lovely and attractive as herself; but towards her husband there was a feeling of instant repulsion. Not that he was coarse or rude in his exterior - that was polished; but there were a sensualism and want of principle about him that could be felt.

They had been in the house only a week or two, when their oldest child, a beautiful boy, was taken ill. He had fever, and complained of distress in his back and pain in his head. The mother appeared anxious, but the father treated the matter lightly, and said he would be well again in a few hours.

"I think you'd better call in a doctor," Mrs. Darlington heard the mother say, as her husband stood at the chamber door ready to go away.

"Nonsense, Jane," he replied. "You are easily frightened. There's nothing serious the matter."

"I'm afraid of scarlet fever, Henry," was answered to this.

"Fiddlesticks! You're always afraid of something," was lightly and unkindly returned.

Mrs. Marion said no more, and her husband went away. About half an hour afterwards, as Mrs. Darlington sat in her room, there was a light tap at her door, which was immediately opened, and Mrs. Marion stepped in. Her face was pale, and it was some moments before her quivering lips could articulate.

"Won't you come up and look at my Willy?" she at length said, in a tremulous voice.

"Certainly, ma'am," replied Mrs. Darlington, rising immediately. "What do you think ails your little boy?"

"I don't know, ma'am; but I'm afraid of scarlet fever - that dreadful disease."

Mrs. Darlington went up to the chamber of Mrs. Marion. On the bed lay Willy, his face flushed with fever, and his eyes wearing a glassy lustre.

"Do you feel sick, my dear?" asked Mrs. Darlington, as she laid her hand on his burning forehead.

"Yes, ma'am," replied the child.

"There are you sick?"

"My head aches."

"Is your throat sore?"

"Yes, ma'am."

"Very sore?"

"It hurts me so that I can hardly swallow."

"What do you think ails him?" asked the mother, in anxious tones.

T.S. Arthur

"It's hard to say, Mrs. Marion; but, if it were my case, I would send for a doctor. Who is your physician?"

"Dr. M -"

"If you would like to have him called in, I will send the waiter to his office."

Mrs. Marion looked troubled and alarmed.

"My husband doesn't think it any thing serious," said she. "I wanted him to go for the doctor."

"Take my advice, and send for a physician," replied Mrs. Darlington.

"If you will send for Dr. M -, I will feel greatly obliged," said Mrs. Marion.

The doctor was sent for immediately. He did not come for two hours, in which time Willy had grown much worse. He looked serious, and answered all questions evasively. After writing a prescription, he gave a few directions, and said he would call again in the evening. At his second visit, he found his patient much worse; and, on the following morning, pronounced it a case of scarlatina.

Already, Willy had made a friend in every member of Mrs. Darlington's family, and the announcement of his dangerous illness was received with acute pain. Miriam took her place beside Mrs. Marion in the sick chamber, all her sympathies alive, and all her fears awakened; and Edith and her mother gave every attention that their other duties in the household would permit.

Rapidly did the disease, which had fixed itself upon the delicate frame of the child, run its fatal course. On the fourth day he died in the arms of his almost frantic mother.

Though Mrs. Marion had been only a short time in the house, yet she had already deeply interested the feelings of Mrs. Darlington and her two eldest daughters, who suffered with her in the affliction almost as severely as if they had themselves experienced a bereavement; and this added to the weight, already painfully oppressive, that rested upon them.

The nearer contact into which the family of Mrs. Darlington and the bereaved mother were brought by this affliction, discovered to the former many things that strengthened the repugnance first felt towards Mr. Marion, and awakened still livelier sympathies for his suffering wife.

One evening, a week after the body of the child was borne out by the mourners and laid to moulder in its kindred dust, the voice of Mr. Marion was heard in loud, angry tones. He was alone with his wife in their chamber. This chamber was next to hat of Edith and Miriam, where they, at the time, happened to be. What he said they could not make out; but they distinctly heard the voice of Mrs. Marion, and the words -

"Oh, Henry! don't! don't!" uttered in tones the most agonizing. They also heard the words, "For the sake of our dear, dear Willy!" used in some appeal.

Both Edith and Miriam were terribly frightened, and sat panting and looking at each other with pale faces.

T.S. Arthur

All now became silent. Not a sound could be heard in the chamber save an occasional low sob. For half an hour this silence continued. Then the door of the chamber was opened, and Marion went down stairs. The closing of the front door announced his departure from the house. Edith and her sister sat listening for some minutes after Marion had left, but not a movement could they perceive in the adjoining chamber.

"Strange! What can it mean?" at length said Miriam, in a husky whisper. Edith breathed heavily to relieve the pressure on her bosom, but made no answer.

"He didn't strike her?" said Miriam, her face growing paler as she made this suggestion.

The moment this was uttered, Edith arose quickly and moved towards the door.

"Where are you going?" asked her sister.

"Into Mrs. Marion's room."

"Oh no, don't!" returned Miriam, speaking from some vague fear that made her heart shrink.

But Edith did not heed the words. Her light tap at Mrs. Marion's door was not answered. Opening it softly, she stepped within the chamber. On the bed, where she had evidently thrown herself, lay Mrs. Marion; and, on approaching and bending over her, Edith discovered that she was sleeping. On perceiving this, she retired as noiselessly as she had entered.

Ten, eleven, twelve o'clock came; and yet Mr. Marion

had not returned. An hour later than this, Edith and her sister lay awake, but up to that time he was still away. On the next morning, when the bell rang for breakfast, and the family assembled at the table, the places of Mr. and Mrs. Marion were vacant. From their nurse it was ascertained that Mr. Marion had not come home since he went out on the evening before, and that his wife had not yet arisen. Between nine and ten o'clock, Mrs. Darlington sent up to know if Mrs. Marion wished any thing, but was answered in the negative. At dinner time Mr. Marion did not make his appearance, and his wife remained in her chamber. Food was sent to her, but it was returned untasted.

During the afternoon, Mrs. Darlington knocked at her door, but the nurse said that Mrs. Marion asked to be excused from seeing her. At supper time food was sent again to her room; but, save part of a cup of tea, nothing was tasted. After tea, Mrs. Darlington called again at her room, but the desire to be excused from seeing her was repeated. Marion did not return that night.

Nearly a week passed, the husband still remaining away, and not once during that time had Mrs. Marion been seen by any member of the family. At the end of this period, she sent word to Mrs. Darlington that she would be glad to see her.

When the latter entered her room, she found her lying upon the bed, with a face so pale and grief-stricken, that she could not help an exclamation of painful surprise.

"My dear madam, what has happened?" said she, as she took her hand.

T.S. Arthur

Mrs. Marion was too much overcome by emotion to be able to speak for some moments. Acquiring self-possession at length, she said, in a low, sad voice -

"My heart is almost broken, Mrs. Darlington. I feel crushed to the very ground. How shall I speak of what I am suffering?"

Her voice quivered and failed. But in a few moments she recovered herself again, and said, more calmly -

"I need not tell you that my husband has been absent for a week; he went away in a moment of anger, vowing that he would never return. Hourly have I waited since, in the hope that he would come back; but, alas! I have thus far received from him neither word nor sign."

Mrs. Marion here gave way to her feelings, and wept bitterly.

"Did he ever leave you before?" asked Mrs. Darlington, as soon as she had grown calm.

"Once."

"How long did he remain away?"

"More than a year."

"Have you friends?"

"I have no relative but an aunt, who is very poor."

Mrs. Darlington sighed involuntarily. On that very day she had been seriously examining into her affairs, and the result was a conviction that, under her present range of expenses, she must go behind-hand with great rapidity. Mr. and Mrs. Marion were to pay fourteen dollars a weeks Thus far, nothing had been received from them; and now the husband had gone off and left his family on her hands. She could not turn them off, yet how could she bear up under this additional burden!

All this passed through her mind in a moment, and produced the sigh which distracted her bosom.

"Do you not know where he has gone?" she asked, seeking to throw as much sympathy and interest in her voice as possible, and thus to conceal the pressure upon her own feelings which the intelligence had occasioned.

Mrs. Marion shook her head. She knew that, in the effort to speak, her voice would fail her.

For nearly the space of a minute there was silence. This was broken, at length, by Mrs. Marion, who again wept violently. As soon as the passionate burst of feeling was over, Mrs. Darlington said to her in a kind and sympathizing voice -

"Do not grieve so deeply. You are not friendless altogether. Though you have been with us only a short time, we feel an interest in you, and will not" -

The sentence remained unfinished. There was an impulse in Mrs. Darlington's mind to proffer the unhappy woman a home for herself and children; but a sudden recollection of the embarrassing nature of her own circumstances checked the words on her tongue.

T.S. Arthur

"I cannot remain a burden upon you," quickly answered Mrs. Marion. "But where can I go? What shall I do?"

The last few words were spoken half to herself, in a low tone of distressing despondency.

"For the present," said Mrs. Darlington, anxious to mitigate, even in a small degree, the anguish of the unhappy woman's mind, "let this give you no trouble. Doubtless the way will open before you. After the darkest hour the morning breaks."

Yet, even while Mrs. Darlington sought thus to give comfort, her own heart felt the weight upon it growing heavier. Scarcely able to stand up in her difficulties alone, here was a new burden laid upon her.

None could have sympathized more deeply with the afflicted mother and deserted wife than did Mrs. Darlington and her family; and none could have extended more willingly a helping hand in time of need. But, in sustaining the burden of her support, they felt that the additional weight was bearing them under.

CHAPTER VI

THREE months more elapsed. Mrs. Marion was still an inmate of the family. Up to this time, not a word had come from her husband, and she had not been able to pay Mrs. Darlington a single dollar.

Painfully did she feel her dependent situation, although she was treated with the utmost delicacy and consideration. But all the widow's means were now exhausted in the payment of the second quarter's rent, and she found her weekly income reduced to thirty-five dollars, scarcely sufficient to meet the weekly expense for supplying the table, paying the servants, etc., leaving nothing for future rent bills, the cost of clothing, and education for the younger children. With all this, Mrs. Darlington's duties had been growing daily more and more severe. Nothing could be trusted to servants that was not, in some way, defectively done, causing repeated complaints from the boarders. What proved must annoying was the bad cooking, to remedy which Mrs. Darlington strove in vain. One day the coffee was not fit to drink, and on the next day the steak would be burnt or broiled as dry as a chip, or the sirloin roasted until every particle of juice had evaporated. If hot cakes were ordered for breakfast, ten chances to one that they were not sour; or, if rolls were baked, they would, most likely, be as heavy as lead.

Such mishaps were so frequent, that the guests of Mrs. Darlington became impatient, and Mr. Scragg, in particular, never let an occasion for grumbling or insolence pass without fully improving it.

"Is your coal out?" said he, one morning, about this

time, as he sat at the breakfast table.

Mrs. Darlington understood, by the man's tone and manner, that he meant to be rude, though she did not comprehend the meaning of the question.

"No, sir," she replied, with some dignity of manner. "Why do you ask?"

"It struck me," he answered, "that such might be the case. But, perhaps, cook is too lazy to bring it out of the cellar. If she'll send for me to-morrow morning, I'll bring her up an extra scuttleful, as I particularly like a good cup of hot coffee."

His meaning was now plain. Quick as thought, the blood rushed to the face of Mrs. Darlington.

She had borne so much from this man, and felt towards him such utter disgust, that she could forbear no longer.

"Mr. Scragg," said she, with marked indignation, "when a gentleman has any complaint to make, he does it as a gentleman."

"Madam!" exclaimed Scragg, with a threat in his voice, while his coarse face became red with anger.

"When a *gentleman* has any complaint to make, he does it *as* a gentleman," repeated Mrs. Darlington, with a more particular emphasis than at first.

"I'd thank you to explain yourself," said Scragg, dropping his hands from the table, and elevating his person.

"My words convey my meaning plainly enough. But, if you cannot understand, I will try to make them clearer. Your conduct is not that of a gentleman."

Of course, Mr. Scragg asked for no further explanation. Starting from the table, he said, looking at Mrs. Scragg -

"Come!"

And Mrs. Scragg arose and followed her indignant spouse.

"Served him right," remarked Burton, in a low voice, bending a little towards Miriam, who sat near him. "I hope we shall now be rid of the low-bred fellow."

Miriam was too much disturbed to make a reply. All at the table felt more or less uncomfortable, and soon retired. Ere dinner time, Mr. and Mrs. Scragg, with their whole brood, had left the house, thus reducing the income of Mrs. Darlington from thirty-five to twenty-three dollars a week.

At dinner time, Mrs. Darlington was in bed. The reaction which followed the excitement of the morning, accompanied as it was with the conviction that, in parting with the Scraggs, insufferable as they were, she had parted with the very means of sustaining herself, completely prostrated her. During the afternoon, she was better, and was able to confer with Edith on the desperate nature of their affairs.

"What are we to do?" said she to her daughter, breaking thus abruptly a silence which had continued for many minutes. "We have an income of only twenty-three dollars a week, and that will scarcely supply the table."

Edith sighed, but did not answer.

"Twenty-three dollars a week," repeated Mrs. Darlington. "What are we to do?"

"Our rooms will not remain vacant long, I hope," said Edith.

"There is little prospect of filling them that I can see," murmured Mrs. Darlington. "If all our rooms were taken, we might get along."

"I don't know," returned Edith to this, speaking thoughtfully. "I sometimes think that our expenses are too great for us to make any thing, even if our rooms were filled. Six hundred dollars is a large rent for us to pay."

"We've sunk three hundred dollars in six months. That is certain," said Mrs. Darlington.

"And our furniture has suffered to an extent almost equivalent," added her daughter.

"Oh, do not speak of that! The thought makes me sick. Our handsome French china dinner set, which cost us a hundred and fifty dollars, is completely ruined. Half of the plates are broken, and there is scarcely a piece of it not injured or defaced. My heart aches to see the destruction going on around us."

"I was in Mr. Scragg's room to-day," said Edith.

"Well, what of it?" asked her mother.

"It would make you sick in earnest to look in there. You know the beautiful bowl and pitcher that were in her chamber?"

"Yes."

"Both handle and spout are off of the pitcher."

"Edith!"

"And the bowl is cracked from the rim to the centre. Then the elegant rosewood washstand is completely ruined. Two knobs are off of the dressing-bureau, the veneering stripped from the edge of one of the drawers, and the whole surface marked over in a thousand lines. It looks as if the children had amused themselves by the hour in scratching it with pins. Three chairs are broken. And the new carpet we put on the floor looks as if it had been used for ten years. Moreover, every thing is in a most filthy condition. It is shocking."

Mrs. Darlington fairly groaned at this intelligence.

"But where is it all to lead, Edith?" she asked, arousing herself from a kind of stupor into which her mind had fallen. "We cannot go on as we are now going."

"We must reduce our expenses, if possible."

"But how are we to reduce them? We cannot send away the cook."

"No. Of course not."

T.S. Arthur

"Nor our chambermaid."

"No. But cannot we dispense with the waiter?"

"Who will attend the table, go to market, and do the dozen other things now required of him?"

"We can get our marketing sent home."

"But the waiting oh the table. Who will do that?"

"Half a dollar a week extra to the chambermaid will secure that service from her."

"But she has enough to do besides waiting on the table," objected Mrs. Darlington.

"Miriam and I will help more through the house than we have yet done. Three dollars a week and the waiter's board will be saving a good deal."

Mrs. Darlington sighed heavily, and then said -

"To think what I have borne from that Scragg and his family, ignorant, low-bred, vulgar people, with whom we have no social affinity whatever, who occupy a level far below us, and who yet put on airs and treat us as if we were only their servants! I could bear his insolence no longer. Ah, to what mortifications are we not subjected in our present position! How little dreamed I of all this, when I decided to open a boarding-house! But, Edith, to come back to what we were conversing about, it would be something to save the expense of our waiter; but what are three or four dollars a week, when we are going behind hand at the rate of twenty?"

"If Mrs. Marion" -

Edith checked herself, and did not say what was in her mind. Mrs. Darlington was silent, sighed again heavily, and then said -

"Yes; if it wasn't for the expense of keeping Mrs. Marion. And she has no claim upon us."

"None but the claim of humanity," said Edith.

"If we were able to pay that claim," remarked Mrs. Darlington.

"True."

"But we are not. Such being the case, are we justified in any longer offering her a home?"

"Where will she go? What will she do?" said Edith.

"Where will we go? What will we do, unless there is a change in our favour?" asked Mrs. Darlington.

"Alas, I cannot tell! When we are weak, small things are felt as a burden. The expense of keeping Mrs. Marion and her two children is not very great. Still, it is an expense that we are unable to meet. But how can we tell her to go?"

"I cannot take my children's bread and distribute it to others," replied Mrs. Darlington, with much feeling. My first duty is to them."

"Poor woman! My heart aches for her," said Edith. "She looks so pale and heart-broken, feels so keenly her state of dependence, and tries so in every possible way to make the pressure of her presence in our family as light as possible, that the very thought of turning her from our door seems to involve cruelty."

"All that, Edith, I feel most sensibly. Ah me! into what a strait are we driven!"

"How many times have I wished that we had never commenced this business!" said Edith. "It has brought us nothing but trouble from the beginning; and, unless my fears are idle, some worse troubles are yet before us."

"Of what kind?"

"Henry did not come home until after two o'clock this morning."

"What!" exclaimed the mother in painful surprise.

"I sat up for him. Knowing that he had gone out with Mr. Barling, and, finding that he had not returned by eleven o'clock, I could not go to bed. I said nothing to Miriam, but sat up alone. It was nearly half past two when he came home in company with Barling. Both, I am sorry to say, were so much intoxicated, that they could scarcely make their way up stairs."

"Oh, Edith!" exclaimed the stricken mother, hiding her face in her hands, and weeping aloud.

Miriam entered the room at this moment, and, seeing her mother in tears, and Edith looking the very image of distress, begged to know the cause of their trouble. Little was said to her then; but Edith, when she was alone with her soon after, fully explained the desperate condition of their affairs. Hitherto they had, out of regard for Miriam, concealed from her the nature of the difficulties that were closing around them.

"I dreamed not of this," said Miriam, in a voice of anguish. "My poor mother! What pain she must suffer! No wonder that her countenance is so often sad. But, Edith, cannot we do something?"

Ever thus, to the mind of the sweet girl, when the troubles of others were mentioned to her, came, first, the desire to afford relief.

"We can do nothing," replied Edith, "at present, unless it be to assist through the house, so that the chambermaid can attend the door, wait on the table, and do other things now required of the waiter."

"And let him go?"

"Yes."

"I am willing to do all in my power, Edith," said Miriam. "But, if mother has lost so much already, will she not lose still more if she continue to go on as she is now going?"

"She hopes to fill all her rooms; then she thinks that she will be able to make something."

"This has been her hope from the first," replied Miriam.

"Yes; and thus far it has been a vain hope."

"Three hundred dollars lost already," sighed Miriam, "our beautiful furniture ruined, and all domestic happiness destroyed! Ah me! Where is all going to end? Uncle Hiram was right when he objected to mother's taking boarders, and said that it was the worst thing she could attempt to do. I wish we had taken his advice. Willingly would I give music lessons or work with my hands for an income, to save mother from the suffering and labour she has now to bear."

"The worst is," said Edith, following out her own thoughts rather than replying to her sister, "now that all our money is gone, debt will follow. How is the next quarter's rent to be paid?"

"A hundred aid fifty dollars?"

"Yes. How can we pay that?"

"Oh dear!" sighed Miriam. What are we to do? How dark all looks!"

"If there is not some change," said Edith, "by the close of another six months, every thing we have will be sold for debt."

"Dreadful!" ejaculated Miriam, "dreadful!"

For a long time the sisters conferred together, but no gleam of light arose in their minds. All the future remained shrouded in darkness.

CHAPTER VII

THE man named Burton, to whom reference has been made as being particularly attentive to Miriam, was really charmed with the beautiful young girl. But the affection of a man such as he was comes to its object as a blight instead of a blessing. Miriam, while she did not repel his attentions, for his manner towards her was ever polite and respectful, felt, nevertheless, an instinctive repugnance towards him, and when she could keep out of his way without seeming to avoid him, she generally did so.

A few evenings after the conversation held with Edith, as given in the last chapter, Burton, in passing from the dining room, said to Miriam, -

"Come. I want you to play for me some of those beautiful airs in Don Giovanni."

"Indeed you must excuse me Mr. Burton," replied Miriam. I don't feel like playing to-night."

"Can't excuse you, indeed," said Burton, smiling pleasantly, and, at the same time, taking Miriam's hand, which she quickly withdrew from his touch. The contact sent an unpleasant thrill along her nerves. "So come. I must have some music to-night."

Miriam yielded to the request, although she felt in no mood for touching the piano. After playing several pieces, she lifted her hands from the instrument, and, turning away from it, said, -

"There, Mr. Burton, you must really excuse me. I

T.S. Arthur

cannot play to-night."

"Excuse you! Certainly. And for the pleasure you have given me, accept my thanks," replied Mr. Burton. There was a change in his tone of voice which Miriam did not comprehend. "And now," he added, in a low voice, bending to her ear, "come and sit down with me on the sofa. I have something particular that I wish to say."

Miriam did as she was desired, not dreaming of what was in the mind of Burton.

"Miriam," said he, after a pause, "do not be startled nor surprised at what I am going to say."

But his words and manner both startled her, and she was about rising, when he took her hand and gently detained her.

"Nay, Miriam," said he, "you must hear what I wish to speak. From the day I entered this house, you have interested me deeply. Admiration was followed quickly by profound respect; and to this succeeded a warmer sentiment."

A deep crimson instantly mantled the face of Miriam, and her eye fell to the floor.

"Can you, my dear young lady," continued Mr. Burton, "reciprocate the feeling I have expressed?"

"Oh, sir! Excuse me!" said Miriam, so soon as she could recover her disordered thoughts. And she made another effort to rise, but was still detained by Burton.

"Stay! stay!" said he. "Hear all that I wish to utter. I am rich" -

But, ere he could speak another word, Miriam sprang from the sofa, and, bounding from the room, flew rather than walked up the stairs. The instant she entered her own room she closed and locked the door, and then, falling upon the bed, gave vent to a flood of tears. A long time passed before her spirit regained its former composure; and then, when her thought turned towards Mr. Burton, she experienced an inward shudder.

Of what had occurred, she breathed not a syllable to Edith when she joined her in the chamber to retire for the night.

"How my heart aches for mother!" sighed Edith, as she came in. "I have been trying to encourage her; but words are of no avail. 'Where is all to end?' she asks; and I cannot answer the question. Oh dear! What is to become of us? At the rate we are going on now, every thing must soon be lost. To think of what we have sacrificed and are still sacrificing, yet all to no purpose. Every comfort is gone. Strangers, who have no sympathy with us, have come into our house; and mother is compelled to bear all manner of indignities from people who are in every way her inferiors. Yet, for all, we are losing instead of gaining. Ah me! No wonder she is heart-sick and utterly discouraged. How could it be otherwise?"

Miriam heard and felt every word; but she made no answer. Thought, however, was busy, and remained busy long after sleep had brought back to the troubled heart of Edith its even pulsations.

T.S. Arthur

"I am rich." These words of Mr. Burton were constantly recurring to her mind. It was in vain that she turned from the idea presented with them: it grew more and more distinct each moment. Yes, there was a way of relief opened for her mother, of safety for the family, and Miriam saw it plainly, yet shuddered as she looked, and closed her eyes, like one about to leap from a fearful height.

Hour after hour Miriam lay awake, pondering the new aspect which things had assumed, and gazing down the fearful abyss into which, in a spirit of self-devotion, she was seeking to find the courage to leap.

"I am rich." Ever and anon these words sounded in her ears. As the wife of Burton, she could at once lift her mother out of her present unhappy situation. Thus, before the hour of midnight came and went, she thought. He had offered her his hand. She might accept the offer, on condition of his settling an income upon her mother.

This the tempter whispered in her ears, and she hearkened, in exquisite pain, to the suggestion.

When Edith awoke on the next morning, Miriam slept soundly by her side; but Edith, observed that her face was pale and troubled, and that tears were on her cheeks. At breakfast time, she did not appear at the table; and when her mother sent to her room she returned for answer that she was not very well. The whole of the day she spent in her chamber, and, during all the time, was struggling against the instinctive repulsion felt towards the man who had made her an offer of marriage.

At supper time, she reappeared at the table with a calm, yet sad face. As she was passing from the dining room after tea, Burton came to her side and whispered-

"Can I have a word with you in the parlour, Miriam?"

The young girl neither looked up nor spoke, but moved along by his side, and descended with him to the parlour, where they were alone.

"Miriam," said Burton, as he placed himself by her side on the sofa, "have you thought seriously of what I said last evening? Can you reciprocate the ardent sentiments I expressed?"

"Oh, sir!" returned Miriam, looking up artlessly in his face, "I am too young to listen to words like these."

"You are a woman, Miriam," replied Burton, earnestly - "a lovely woman, with a heart overflowing with pure affections. Deeply have you interested my feelings from the first; and now I ask you to be mine. As I was going to say last evening, I am rich, and will surround you with every comfort and elegance that money can obtain. Dearest Miriam, say that you will accept the hand I now offer you."

"My mother will never consent," said the trembling girl, after a long pause.

"Your mother is in trouble. I have long seen that," remarked Mr. Burton, "and have long wanted to advise and befriend her. Put it in my power to do so, and then ask for her what you will."

This was touching the right key, and Burton saw it in

a moment.

"Yes, you have said truly," replied Miriam; "my mother is in great trouble. Ah! what would I not do for her relief?"

"Ask for your mother what you will, Miriam," said Burton.

The maiden's eyes were upon the floor, and the rapid heaving of her bosom showed that her thoughts were busy in earnest debate. At length, looking up, she said -

"Will you lift her out of her present embarrassed position, and settle upon her an income sufficient for herself and family?"

"I will," was the prompt answer. "And now, my dear Miriam, name the sum you wish her to receive."

Another long silence followed.

"Ah, sir!" at length said the maiden, "in what a strange, humiliating position am I placed!"

"Do not speak thus, Miriam. I understand all better than words can utter it. Will an income of two thousand dollars a year suffice?"

"It is more than I could ask."

"Enough. The moment you are mine, that sum will be settled on your mother."

Miriam arose up quickly, as Burton said this, murmuring -

"Let me have a few days for reflection," and, ere he could prevent her, glided from the room.

T.S. Arthur

Two weeks more went by, and the pressure upon Mrs. Darlington was heavier and heavier. Her income was below her table expenses and servant-hire, and all her reserve fund being exhausted, she felt the extremity of her circumstances more than at any time before. To bear longer the extra weight of poor, deserted Mrs. Marion and her two children was felt to be impossible. With painful reluctance did Mrs. Darlington slowly make up her mind to say to Mrs. Marion that she must seek another home; and for this purpose she one day waited upon her in her room. As tenderly and as delicately as possible did she approach the subject. A word or two only had she said, when Mrs. Marion, with tears upon her face, replied, -

"Pardon me that I have so long remained a burden upon you. Had I known where to go, or what to do, I would not have added my weight to the heavy ones you have had to bear. Daily have I lived in hope that my husband would return. But my heart is sick with hope deferred. It is time now that I began the work of self-dependence."

"Where can you go?" asked Mrs. Darlington.

"I know not," sadly returned Mrs. Marion. "My only relative is a poor aunt, with scarcely the ability to support herself. But I will see her to-day. Perhaps she can advise me what to do."

When Mrs. Marion returned from this visit to her aunt, she looked very sad. Mrs. Darlington was in the passage as she came in; but she passed her without speaking, and hurried up to her chamber. Neither at tea time on that evening nor at breakfast time on the next morning did she appear, though food for herself and children was sent to her room. Deeply did Mrs. Darlington and her daughters suffer on account of the step they were compelled to take, but stern necessity left them no alternative. During the day, Mrs. Marion went out again for an hour or two, and when she came back she announced that she would leave on the next day. She looked even sadder than before. Some inquiries as to where she was going were made, but she evaded them. On the day following, a carriage came for her, and she parted with her kind friends, uttering the warmest expressions of gratitude.

"I have turned her from the house!" said Mrs. Darlington, in a tone of deep regret, as she closed the door upon the poor creature. "How would I like my own child treated thus?"

For the rest of the day she was so unhappy, owing to this circumstance, that she could scarcely attend to any thing.

"Do you know where Mrs. Marion went when she left our house?" said Edith to her mother, about two weeks afterwards. There was a troubled look in Edith's face as she asked this question.

"No. Where is she?"

"At Blockley."

"What!"

"In the Alms-house!"

T.S. Arthur

"Edith!"

"It is too true. I have just learned that when she left here, it was to take up her abode among paupers. She had no other home."

Mrs. Darlington clasped her hands together, and was about giving expression to her feelings, when a domestic came in and said that Mr. Ellis was in the parlour, and wished to see her immediately.

"Where is Miriam?" asked the brother, in a quick voice, the moment Mrs. Darlington entered the parlour, where he awaited her.

"She's in her room, I believe. Why do you ask?"

"Are you certain? Go up, Edith, quickly, and see."

The manner of Mr. Ellis was so excited that Edith did not pause to hear more, but flew up stairs. In a few moments she returned, saying that her sister was not there, and that, moreover, on looking into her drawers, she found them nearly empty.

"Then it was her!" exclaimed Mr. Ellis.

"Where is she? Where did you see her?" eagerly asked both mother and sister, their faces becoming as pale as ashes.

"I saw her in a carriage with a notorious gambler and scoundrel named Burton. There was a trunk on behind, and they were driving towards the wharf. It is ten minutes before the boat starts for New York, and I may save her yet!"

And, with these words, Mr. Ellis turned abruptly away, and hurried from the house. So paralyzed were both Mrs. Darlington and Edith by this dreadful announcement, that neither of them had for a time the power of utterance. Then both, as by a common impulse, arose and went up to the chamber where Miriam slept. Almost the first thing that met the eyes of Mrs. Darlington was a letter, partly concealed by a book on the mantel-piece. It was addressed to her. On breaking the seal, she read -

"MY DEAR, DEAR MOTHER: I shall be away from you only a little while; and, when I return, I will come with relief for all your present troubles. Do not blame me, dear mother! What I have done is for your sake. It almost broke my heart to see you so pressed down and miserable. And, then, there was no light ahead. Mr. Burton, who has great wealth, offered me his hand. Only on condition of a handsome settlement upon you would I accept of it. Forgive me that I have acted without consultation. I deemed it best. In a little while, I will be back to throw myself into your arms, and then to lift you out of your many troubles. How purely and tenderly I love you, mother, dear mother! I need not say. It is from this love that I am now acting. Take courage, mother. Be comforted. We shall yet be happy. Farewell, for a little while. In a few days I will be with you again.

"MIRIAM."

As Mrs. Darlington read the last sentence of this letter, Henry, her son, who had not been home since he went out at breakfast-time, came hurriedly into the room,

T.S. Arthur

and, in an excited manner, said -

"Mother, I want ten dollars!"

The face of the young man was flushed, and his eyes unsteady. It was plain, at a glance, that he had been drinking.

Mrs. Darlington looked at him for a moment, and then, before Edith had seen the contents of Miriam's letter, placed it in his hands.

"What does this mean?" he exclaimed, after running his eyes over it hurriedly. "Miriam gone off with that Burton!"

The letter dropped upon the floor, and Henry clasped his hands together with a gesture of pain.

"Who is Mr. Burton? What do you know of him?" asked Edith.

"I know him to be a man of the vilest character, and a gambler into the bargain! Rich! Gracious heaven!"

And the young man struck his hands against his forehead, and glanced wildly from his pale-faced mother to his paler sister.

"And you knew the character of this man, Henry!" said Mrs. Darlington. There was a smiting rebuke in her tone. "You knew him, and did not make the first effort to protect your young, confiding, devoted sister! Henry Darlington, the blood of her murdered happiness will never be washed from the skirts of your garments!"

"Mother! mother!" exclaimed the young man, putting up his hands to enforce the deprecation in his voice, "do not speak so, or I will go beside myself! But where is she? When did she go? I will fly in pursuit. It may not yet be too late."

"Your Uncle Hiram saw her in a carriage with Mr. Burton, on their way, as he supposed, to the steamboat landing. He has gone to intercept them, if possible."

Henry drew his watch from his pocket, and, as he glanced at the time, sank into a chair, murmuring, in a low voice of anguish -

"It is too late!"

CHAPTER IX

WHEN Mr. Ellis left the house of his sister, he called a carriage that happened to be going by, and reached the wharf at Walnut street in time. to spring on board of the steamboat just as the plank was drawn in at the gangway. He then passed along the boat until he came to the ladies' cabin, which he entered. Almost the first persons he saw were Burton and his niece. The eyes of Miriam rested upon him at the same moment, and she drew her veil quickly, hoping that she was not recognised. Hiram Ellis did not hesitate a moment, but, walking up to where Miriam sat, stooped to her ear, and said, in a low, anxious voice -

"Miriam, are you married yet?"

Miriam did not reply.

"Speak, child. Are you married?"

"No," came in a half audible murmur.

"Thank God! thank God!" fell in low accents from the lips of Mr. Ellis.

"Who are you, sir?" now spoke up Burton, whom surprise had till now kept silent. There was a fiery gleam in his eyes.

"The uncle of this dear girl, and one who knows you well," was answered, in a stern voice. "Knows you to be unworthy to touch even the hem of her garment."

A dark scowl lowered upon the face of Burton. But

Mr. Ellis returned his looks of anger glance for glance. Miriam was in terror at this unexpected scene, and trembled like an aspen. Instinctively she shrank towards her uncle.

Two or three persons, who sat near, were attracted by the excitement visible in the manner of all three, although they heard nothing that was said. Burton saw that they were observed, and, bending towards Mr. Ellis, said -

"This, sir, is no place for a scene. A hundred eyes will soon be upon us."

"More than one pair of which," replied Mr. Ellis, promptly, "will recognise in you a noted gambler, who has at least one wife living, if no more."

As if stung by a serpent, Burton started to his feet and retired from the cabin.

"Oh, uncle! can what you say of this man be true?" asked Miriam, with a blanching face.

"Too true, my dear child! too true! He is one of the worst of men. Thank God that you have escaped the snare of the fowler!"

"Yes, thank God! thank God!" came trembling from the lips of the maiden.

Mr. Ellis then drew his niece to a part of the cabin where they could converse without being overheard by other passengers on board of the boat. To his inquiry into the reasons for so rash an act, Miriam gave her uncle an undisguised account of her mother's distressed condition, and touchingly portrayed the anguish of mind which had accompanied her reluctant assent to the offer of Burton.

"And all this great sacrifice was on your mother's account?" said Mr. Ellis.

"All! all! He agreed to settle upon her the sum of two thousand dollars a year, if I would become his wife. This would have made the family comfortable."

"And you most wretched. Better, a thousand times better, have gone down to your grave, Miriam, than become the wife of that man. But for the providential circumstance of my seeing you in the carriage with him, all would have been lost. Surely, you could not have felt for him the least affection."

"Oh, uncle! you can never know what a fearful trial I have passed through. Affection! It was, instead, an intense repugnance. But, for my mother's sake, I was prepared to make any sacrifice consistent with honour."

"Of all others, my dear child," said Mr. Ellis, with much feeling, "a sacrifice of this kind is the worst. It is full of evil consequences that cannot be enumerated, and scarcely imagined. You had no affection for this man, and yet, in the sight of Heaven, you were going solemnly to vow that you would love and cherish him through life!"

A shudder ran through the frame of Miriam, which being perceived by Mr. Ellis, he said -

"Well may you shudder, as you stand looking down the

awful abyss into which you were about plunging. You can see no bottom, and you would have found none. There is no condition in this life, Miriam, so intensely wretched as that of a pure-minded, true-hearted woman united to a man whom she not only cannot love, but from whom every instinct of her better nature turns with disgust. And this would have been your condition. Ah me! in what a fearful evil was this error of your mother, in opening a boarding-house, about involving her child! I begged her not to do so. I tried to show her the folly of such a step. But she would not hear me. And now she is in great trouble?"

"Oh yes, uncle. All the money she had when she began is spent; and what she now receives from boarders but little more than half pays expenses."

"I knew it would be so. But my word was not regarded. Your mother is no more fitted to keep a boarding-house than a child ten years old. It takes a woman who has been raised in a different school, who has different habits, and a different character."

"But what can we do, uncle?" said Miriam.

"What are you willing to do?"

"I am willing to do any thing that is right for me to do."

"All employment, Miriam, are honourable so far as they are useful," said Mr. Ellis, seriously, "though false pride tries to make us think differently. And, strangely enough, this false pride drives too many, in the choice of employments, to the hardest, least honourable, and least profitable. hundreds of women resort to keeping boarders as a means of supporting their families when they might do it more easily, with less exposure and greater certainty, in teaching, if qualified, fine needle-work, or even in the keeping of a store for the sale of fancy and useful articles. But pursuits of the latter kind they reject as too far below them, and, in vainly attempting to keep up a certain appearance, exhaust what little means they have. A breaking up of the family, and a separation of its members, follow the error in too many cases."

Miriam listened to this in silence. Her uncle paused.

"What can I do to aid my mother?" the young girl asked.

"Could you not give music lessons?"

"I am too young, I fear, for that. Too little skilled in the principles of music," replied Miriam.

"If competent, would you object to teach?"

"Oh, no. Most gladly would I enter upon the task, did it promise even a small return. How happy would it make me if I could lighten, by my own labour, the burdens that press so heavily upon our mother!"

"And Edith. How does she feel on this subject?"

"As I do. Willing for any thing; ready for any change from our present condition."

"Take courage, then, my dear child, take courage," said the uncle, in a cheerful voice. "There is light ahead."

"Oh, how distressed my mother will be when she finds I am gone!" sighed Miriam, after a brief silence, in which her thoughts reverted to the fact of her absence from home. "When can we get back again?"

"Not before ten o'clock to-night. We must go on as far as Bristol, and then return by the evening line from New York."

Another deep sigh heaved the troubled bosom of Miriam, as she uttered, in a low voice, speaking to herself -

"My poor mother! Her heart will be broken!"

T.S. Arthur

CHAPTER X

MEANWHILE the hours passed with the mother, sister, and brother in the most agonizing suspense. Henry, who had been drawn away into evil company by two young men who boarded in the house, was neglecting his studies, and pressing on towards speedy ruin. To drinking and association with the vicious, he now added gaming. Little did his mother dream of the perilous ways his feet were treading. On this occasion he had come in, as has been seen, with a demand for ten dollars. When he left home in the morning, it was in company with the young man named Barling. Instead of his going to the office where he was studying, or his companion to his place of business, they went to a certain public house in Chestnut Street, where they first drank at the bar.

"Shall we go up into the billiard-room?" said Barling, as they turned from the white marble counter at which they had been drinking.

"I don't care. Have you time to play a game?" replied Henry.

"Oh, yes. We're not very busy at the store to-day."

So the two young men ascended to the billiard-room, and spent a couple of hours there. Both played very well, and were pretty equally matched.

From the billiard-room, they proceeded to another part of the house, more retired, and there, at the suggestion of Barling, tried a game at cards for a small stake. Young Darlington was loser at first, but, after a time, regained his losses and made some advance on his fellow-player. Hours passed in playing and drinking; and finally, Darlington, whose good fortune did not continue, parted with every sixpence.

"Lend me a dollar," said he as the last game went against him.

The dollar was lent, and the playing renewed. Thus it went on, hour after hour, neither of the young men stopping to eat any thing, though both drank too frequently. At last, Darlington was ten dollars in debt to Barling, who, on being asked for another loan, declined any further advances. Stung by the refusal, Henry said to him, rising as he spoke -

"Do you mean by this that you are afraid I will never return the money?"

"Oh, no," replied Barling. "But I don't want to play against you any longer. Your luck is bad."

"I can beat you," said Darlington.

"You hav'n't done it to-day certainly," answered Barling.

"Will you wait here a quarter of an hour?" asked Henry.

"For what?"

"I want to pay you off and begin again. I am going for some money."

"Yes, I'll wait," replied the young man.

"Very well. I'll be back in a few minutes."

It was for this work and for this purpose that Henry Darlington came to his mother just at the moment the absence of Miriam and her purpose in leaving had been discovered. The effect of the painful news on the young man has already been described. From the time he became aware of the fact that Miriam had gone away with Burton for the purpose of becoming his wife, until ten o'clock at night, he was in an agony of suspense. As the uncle could not be found at the office where he wrote, nor at the house where he boarded, it was concluded that he had reached the boat before its departure, and gone on with the fugitives in the train to New York. Nothing was therefore left for the distressed family but to await his return.

How anxiously passed the hours! At tea time Edith only made her appearance. Henry and his mother remained in the chamber of the latter. As for the young man, he was cast down and distressed beyond measure, vexing his spirit with self-accusations that were but too well founded.

"Oh, mother!" said he, while they were alone, starting up from where he had been sitting with his face buried in his hands - "oh, mother! what evils have come through this opening of our house, for strangers to enter! Miriam, our sweet, gentle, pure-hearted Miriam, has been lured away by one of the worst of men; and!" - the young man checked himself a moment or two, and then continued - "and I have been drawn away from right paths into those that lead to sure destruction. Mother, I have been in great danger. Until Barling and Mason came into our family, I was guiltless of any act that could awaken a blush of shame upon my cheek.

Oh, that I had never met them!"

"Henry! Henry! what do you mean by this?" exclaimed Mrs. Darlington, in a voice full of anguish.

"I have been standing on the brink of a precipice," replied the young man with more calmness. "But a hand has suddenly drawn me away, and I am trembling at the danger I have escaped. Oh, mother, will you not give up this mode of life? We have none of us been happy. I have never felt as if I had a home since it began. And you - what a slave have you been! and how unhappy! Can nothing be done except keeping boarders? Oh, what would I not give for the dear seclusion of a home where no stranger's foot could enter!"

"Some other mode of living must be sought, my son," replied Mrs. Darlington. "Added to all the evils attendant on the present mode, is that of a positive loss instead of a profit. Several hundred dollars have been wasted already, and daily am I going in debt."

"Then, mother, let us change at once," replied the young man. "It would be better to shrink together in a single room than to continue as we are. I will seek a clerkship in a store and earn what I can to help support the family."

"I can think of nothing now but Miriam!" said Mrs. Darlington. "Oh, if she were back again, safe from the toils that have been thrown around her, I think I would be the most thankful of mortals! Oh, my child! my child!"

What could Henry say to comfort his mother? Nothing.

T.S. Arthur

And he remained silent.

Long after this, Mrs. Darlington, with Henry and Edith, were sitting together in painful suspense. No word had been spoken by either for the space of nearly an hour. The clock struck ten.

"I would give worlds to see my dear, dear child!" murmured Mrs. Darlington.

Just then a carriage drove up to the door and stopped. Henry sprang down stairs; but neither Edith nor her mother could move from where they sat. As the former opened the street door, Miriam stood with her uncle on the threshold. Henry looked at her earnestly and tenderly for an instant, and then, staggering back, leaned against the wall for support.

"Where is your mother?" asked Mr. Ellis.

"In her own room," said Henry, in a voice scarcely audible.

Miriam sprang up the stairs with the fleetness of an antelope, and, in a few moments, was sobbing on her mother's bosom.

"Miriam! Miriam!" said Mrs. Darlington, in a thrilling voice, "do you return the same as when you left?"

"Yes, thank God!" came from the maiden's lips.

"Thank God! thank God!" responded the mother, wildly. "Oh, my child, what a fearful misery you have escaped!"

In a few minutes, the mother and sisters were joined by Henry.

"Where is your uncle?" asked Mrs. Darlington.

"He has gone away; but says that he will see you to-morrow."

Over the remainder of that evening we will here draw a veil.

T.S. Arthur

CHAPTER XI

ON the next morning, only Mrs. Darlington met her boarders at the breakfast-table, when she announced to them that she had concluded to close her present business, and seek some new mode of sustaining her family; at the same time, desiring each one to find another home as early as possible.

At the close of the third day after this, Mrs. Darlington sat down to her evening meal with only her children gathered at the table. A subdued and tranquil spirit pervaded each bosom, even though a dark veil was drawn against the future. To a long and troubled excitement there had succeeded a calm. It was good to be once more alone, and they felt this. "Through what a scene of trial, disorder, and suffering have we passed!" said Edith. "It seems as if I had just awakened from a dream."

"And such a dream!" sighed Miriam.

"Would that it were but a dream!" said Mrs. Darlington. "But, alas! the wrecks that are around us too surely testify the presence of a devastating storm."

"The storm has passed away, mother," said Edith; "and we will look for calmer and brighter skies."

"No bright skies for us, I fear, my children," returned the mother, with a deeper tinge of sadness in her voice.

"They are bright this hour to what they were a few days since," said Edith, "and I am sure they will grow brighter. I feel much encouraged. Where the heart is willing, the way is sure to open. Both Miriam and I are willing to do all in our power, and I am sure we can do much. We have ability to teach others; and the exercise of that ability will bring a sure reward. I like Uncle Hiram's suggestion very much."

"But the humiliation of soliciting scholars," said the mother.

"To do right is not humiliating," quickly replied Edith.

"It is easy to say this, my child; but can you go to Mrs. Lionel, for instance, with whose family we were so intimate, and solicit her to send Emma and Cordelia to the school you propose to open, without a smarting sense of humiliation? I am sure you cannot."

Edith communed with her own thoughts for some moments, and then answered -

"If I gave way to false pride, mother, this might be so; but I must overcome what is false and evil. This is as necessary for my happiness as the external good we seek - nay, far more so. Too many who have moved in the circle where we have been moving for years strangely enough connect an idea of degradation with the office of teaching children. But is there on the earth a higher or more important use than instructing the mind and training the heart of young immortals? It has been beautifully and truly said, that 'Earth is the nursery of Heaven.' The teacher, then, is a worker in God's own garden. Is it not so, mother?"

"You think wisely, my child. God grant that your true thoughts may sustain you in the trials to come!" replied Mrs. Darlington.

T.S. Arthur

The door-bell rang as the family were rising from the tea-table. The visitor was Mr. Ellis. He had come to advise with and assist the distressed mother and her children; and his words were listened to with far more deference than was the case a year before. Nine or ten months' experience in keeping a boarding-house had corrected many of the false views of Mrs. Darlington, and she was now prepared to make an effort for her family in a different spirit from that exhibited in the beginning. The plan proposed by her brother - a matter-of-fact kind of person - was the taking of a house at a more moderate rent, and opening a school for young children. Many objections and doubts were urged; but he overruled them all, and obtained, in the end, the cordial consent of every member of the family. During the argument which preceded the final decision of the matter, Mrs. Darlington said -

"Suppose the girls should not be able to get scholars?"

"Let them see to this beforehand."

"Many may promise to send, and afterwards change their minds."

"Let them," replied the brother. "If, at the end of the first, second, and third years, you have not made your expenses, I will supply the deficiency."

"You!"

"Yes. The fact is, sister, if you will be guided in some respects by my judgment, I will stand by you, and see you safely over every difficulty. Your boarding-house experiment I did not approve. I saw from the beginning how it would end, and I wished to see the end as quickly as possible. It has come, and I am glad of it; and, still further, thankful that the disaster has not been greater. If you only had now the five or six hundred dollars wasted in a vain experiment during the past year, how much the sum might do for you! But we will not sigh over this. As just said, I will stand by you in the new experiment, and see that you do not fall again into embarrassment."

Henry was present at this interview, but remained silent during the whole time. Since the day of Miriam's departure with Burton, and safe return, a great change had taken place in the young man. He was like one starting up from sleep on the brink of a fearful precipice, and standing appalled at the danger he had escaped almost by a miracle. The way in which he had begun to walk he saw to be the way to sure destruction, and his heart shrunk with shame and trembled with dismay.

"Henry," said the uncle, after an hour's conversation with his sister and Edith, "I would like to talk with you alone."

Mrs. Darlington and her daughters left the room.

"Henry," said Mr. Ellis, as soon as the rest had withdrawn, "you are old enough to do something to help on. All the burden ought not to come on Edith and Miriam."

"Only show me what I can do, uncle, and I am ready to put my hands to the work," was Henry's prompt reply.

"It will be years before you can expect an income from your profession."

"I know, I know. That is what discourages me."

"I can get you the place of clerk in an insurance office, at a salary of five hundred dollars a year. Will you accept it?"

"Gladly!" The face of the young man brightened as if the sun had shone upon it suddenly.

"You will have several hours each day, in which to continue your law reading, and will get admitted to the bar early enough. Keep your mother and sisters for two or three years, and then they will be in a condition to sustain you until you make a practice in your profession."

But to this the mother and sisters, when it was mentioned to them, objected. They were not willing to have Henry's professional studies interrupted. That would be a great wrong to him.

"Not a great wrong, but a great good," answered Mr. Ellis. "And I will make this plain to you. Henry, as I learn from yourself, has made some dangerous associations; and some important change is needed to help him break away from them. No sphere of life is so safe for a young man as that which surrounds profitable industry pursued for an end. Temptation rarely finds its way within this sphere. Two or three years devoted to the duties of a clerk, with the end of aiding in the support of his mother and sisters, will do more to give a right direction to Henry's character - more to make success in after life certain - than any thing else possible now to be done. The office in which I can get him the situation I speak of adjoins the one to which I am attached, and I will, therefore, have him mostly under my own eye. In this new school, the ardency of his young feelings will be duly chastened, and his thoughts turned more into elements of usefulness. In a word, sister, it will give him self-dependence, and, in the end, make a man of him."

The force of all this, and more by this suggested, was not only seen, but felt, by Mrs. Darlington; and when she found her son ready to accept the offer made to him, she withdrew all opposition.

Steps preliminary to the contemplated change were immediately taken. First of all, Edith waited upon a number of their old friends, who had young children, and informed them that she was, in connection with her sister, about opening a school. Some were surprised, some pleased, and some indifferent at the announcement; but a goodly number expressed pleasure at the opportunity it afforded them of placing their younger children under the care of teachers in whose ability and character they had so much confidence. Thus was the way made plain before them.

T.S. Arthur

CHAPTER XII

A FEW weeks later, and the contemplated change was made. The family removed into a moderate-sized house, at a lower rent, and prepared to test the new mode of obtaining a livelihood. A good portion of their furniture had been sold, besides three gold watches and some valuable jewelry belonging to Mrs. Darlington and her two eldest daughters, in order to make up a sum sufficient to pay off the debt contracted during the last few months of the boarding-house experiment. The real loss sustained by the widow in this experiment fell little short of a thousand dollars.

"How many scholars have you now?" asked Mrs. Darlington of Edith, two months after the school was opened, as they sat at tea one evening, each member of the family wearing a cheerful face.

"Twenty," replied Edith. "We received two new ones to-day. Mrs. Wilmot came and entered two of her children; and she said that Mrs. Armond was going to send her Florence so soon as her quarter expired in the school she is now attending."

"How much will you receive from your present number of scholars?" inquired Henry.

"I made the estimate to-day," returned Edith, "and find that the bills will come to something like a hundred and twenty-five dollars a quarter."

"Five hundred dollars a year," said Henry; "and my five hundred added to that will make a thousand. Can't we live on a thousand dollars, mother?"

"We may, by the closest economy."

"Our school will increase," remarked Edith; and every increase will add to our income. Oh! it looks so much brighter ahead! and we have so much real comfort in the present! What a scene of trial have we passed through!"

"How I ever bore up under it is more than I can now tell," said Mrs. Darlington, with an involuntary shudder. "And the toil, and suffering, and danger through which we have come! I cannot be sufficiently thankful that we are safe from the dreadful ordeal, and with so few marks of the fire upon us."

A silence followed this, in which two hearts, at least, were humbled, yet thankful, in their self-communion - the hearts of Henry and Miriam. Through what perilous ways had they come! How near had they been to shipwreck!

"Poor Mrs. Marion!" said Edith, breaking the silence, at length. "How often I think of her! And the thought brings a feeling of condemnation. Was it right for us to thrust her forth as we did?"

"Can she still be in?"

"Oh no, no!" spoke up Henry, interrupting his mother. I forgot to tell you that I met her and her husband on the street to-day."

"Are you certain?"

"Oh yes."

"Did you speak to them?"

"No. They saw me, but instantly averted their faces. Mrs. Marion looked very pale, as if she had been sick."

"Poor woman! She has had heart-sickness enough," said Mrs. Darlington. "I shall never forgive myself for turning her out of the house. If I had known where she was going!"

"But we did not know that, mother," said Edith.

"We knew that she had neither friends nor a home," replied the mother. "Ah me! when our own troubles press heavily upon us, we lose our sympathy for others!"

"It was not so in this case," remarked Edith. "Deeply did we sympathize with Mrs. Marion. But we could not bear the weight without going under ourselves."

"I don't know, I don't know," said Mrs. Darlington, half to herself. "We might have kept up with her a little longer. But I am glad from my heart that her husband has come back. If he will be kind to his wife, I will forgive all his indebtedness to me."

A few weeks subsequent to this time, as Miriam sat reading the morning paper, she came upon a brief account of the arrest, in New Orleans, of a "noted gambler," as it said, named Burton, on the charge of bigamy. The paper dropped to the floor, and Miriam, with clasped hands and eyes instantly overflowing with tears, looked upward, and murmured her thanks to Heaven.

"What an escape!" fell tremblingly from her lips, as she arose and went to her room to hold communion with her own thoughts.

Three years have passed, and what has been the result of the widow's new experiment? The school prospered from the beginning. The spirit with which Edith and Miriam went to work made success certain. Parents who sent their children were so much pleased with the progress they made, that they spoke of the new school to their friends, and thus gave it a reputation, that, ere a year had elapsed, crowded the rooms of the sisters. Mrs. Darlington was a woman who had herself received a superior education. Seeing that the number of scholars increased rapidly, and made the pressure on her daughters too great, she gave a portion of her time each day to the instruction of certain classes, and soon became much interested in the work. From that time she associated herself in the school with Edith and Miriam.

Three years, as we said, have passed, and now the profits on the school are more than sufficient to meet all expenses. Henry has left his clerkship, and is a member of the bar. Of course he has little or no practice - only a few months having elapsed since his admission; but his mother and sisters are fully able to sustain him until he could sustain himself.

"How much better this is than keeping boarders!" said Edith, as she sat conversing with her mother and uncle about the prospects of the school.

"And how much more useful and honourable!" remarked Mr. Ellis. "In the one case, you fed only the body, but now you are dispensing food to the immortal mind. You are moreover independent in your own house. When the day's work is done, you come together as one family, and shut out the intruding world."

"Yes, it is better, far better," replied Mrs. Darlington. "Ah, that first mistake of mine was a sad one!"

"Yet out of it has come good," said Mr. Ellis. "That painful experience corrected many false views, and gave to all your characters a new and higher impulse. It is through disappointment, trial, and suffering, that we grow wise here; and true wisdom is worth the highest price we are ever called upon to pay for it."

Yes, it is so. Through fiery trials are we purified. At times, in our suffering, we feel as if every good thing in us was about being consumed. But this never happens. No good in our characters is ever lost in affliction or trouble; and we come out of these states of pain wiser and better than when we entered them, and more fitted and more willing to act usefully our part in the world.

PLAIN SEWING; OR,
HOW TO ENCOURAGE THE POOR

"Do you know of any poor body who does plain sewing?" asked Mrs. Lander of a neighbour upon whom she called for the particular purpose of making this inquiry. "I have a good deal of work that I want done, and I always like to give my plain sewing to people that need it."

"I think I know of a person who will suit you," replied Mrs. Brandon, the lady to whom the application had been made. "She is a poor widow woman, with four children dependent upon her for support. She sews neatly. Yesterday she brought me home some little drawers and night-gowns that were beautifully made. I am sure she will please you, and I know she deserves encouragement."

"What is her name?"

"Mrs. Walton; and she lives in Larkin's Court."

"Thank you, ma'am. I will send for her this morning. You say she is very poor?"

"You may judge of that yourself, Mrs. Lander. A woman who has four children to support by the labour of her own hands cannot be very well off."

122   T.S. Arthur

"No - certainly not. Poor creature! I will throw all I can in her way, if her work should please me."

"I am sure that will be the case, for she sews very neatly."

Mrs. Lander having found out a poor woman who could do plain sewing - she was always more ready to employ persons in extreme poverty than those who were in more easy circumstances - immediately sent a summons for her to attend upon her ladyship. Mrs. Walton's appearance, when she came, plainly enough told the story of her indigence.

"Mrs. Brandon informs me," said Mrs. Lander, "that you do plain sewing very well, and that you stand in need of work. I always like to encourage the industrious poor."

The woman inclined her head, and Mrs. Lander went on.

"Do you make shirts?"

"Yes, ma'am, sometimes."

"Do you consider yourself a good shirt maker?"

"I don't call myself any thing very extra; but people for whom I work seem generally pleased with what I do."

"I have six shirts cut out for Mr. Lander. How soon can you make them?"

"I couldn't make them all in less than a couple of weeks, as I have other work that must be done within that time."

"Very well. That will do."

The poor woman took the shirts home, feeling grateful to Mrs. Brandon for having recommended her, and thankful to get the work. In order to give satisfaction to both her new customer, and those for whom she already had work in the house, she divided her time between them, sewing one day for Mrs. Lander and the next on the work received before hers came in. At the end of a week, three of the shirts were ready, and, as she needed very much the money she had earned in making them, she carried them over to Mrs. Lander on Saturday afternoon.

"I have three of the shirts ready," said she, as she handed to the lady the bundle she had brought.

"Ah! have you?" remarked Mrs. Lander, as, with a grave face, she opened the bundle and examined the garments. This examination was continued with great minuteness, and long enough almost to have counted every stitch in the garments. She found the shirts exceedingly well made; much better than she had expected to find them.

"When will you have the others ready?" she asked, as she laid them aside.

"I will try and bring them in next Saturday."

"Very well."

Then came a deep silence. The poor woman sat with the, fingers of both hands moving together uneasily, and Mrs. Lander looked away out of the window and appeared to be intent upon something in the street.

"Are these made to please you?" Mrs. Walton ventured to ask.

"They'll do," was the brief answer; and then came the same dead silence, and the same interest on the part of the lady in something passing in the street.

Mrs. Walton wanted the money she had earned for making the shirts, and Mrs. Lander knew it.

But Mrs. Lander never liked to pay out money, if she could help it; and as doing so always went against the grain, it was her custom to put off such unpleasant work as long as possible. She liked to encourage the very poor, because she knew they generally worked cheaper than people who were in easier circumstances; but the drawback in their case was, that they always wanted money the moment their work was done.

Badly as she stood in need of the money she had earned, poor Mrs. Walton felt reluctant to ask for it until the whole number of shirts she had engaged to make were done; and so, after sitting for a little while longer, she got up and went away. It happened that she had expended her last sixpence on that very morning, and nothing was due to her from any one but Mrs. Lander. Two days at least would elapse before she would have any other work ready to take home, and what to do in the mean time she did not know. With her the reward of every day's labour was needed when the labour was done; but now she was unpaid for full four days' work, and her debtor was a lady much interested in the welfare of the poor, who always gave out her plain sewing to those who were in need of encouragement.

By placing in pawn some few articles of dress, and paying a heavy interest upon the little sum of money advanced thereon, the poor widow was able to keep hunger from her door until she could finish some work she had in hand for a lady more considerate than Mrs. Lander. Then she applied herself with renewed industry to the three shirts yet to make, which she finished at the time she promised to have them done. With the money to be received for these, she was to pay one dollar and a half to get her clothes from the pawnbroker's shop, buy her little boy a pair of shoes, - he had been from school a week for want of them, - and get a supply of food for the many mouths she had to feed.

Mrs. Lander received her with that becoming dignity of manner and gravity which certain persons always assume when money has to be paid out. She, as it behooved her to do, thoroughly examined every seam, line of stitching, and hem upon each of the three shirts, and then, after slowly laying the garments upon a table sighed, and looked still graver. Poor Mrs. Walton felt oppressed; she hardly knew why.

"Does the work please you?" she ventured to ask.

"I don't think these are as well made as the others," said Mrs. Lander.

"I thought they were better made," returned the woman.

"Oh, no. The stitching on the bosoms, collars, and

wristbands isn't nearly so well done."

Mrs. Walton knew better than this; but she did not feel in any humour to contend for the truth. Mrs. Lander took up the shirts again, and made another examination.

"What is the price of them?" she asked.

"Seventy-five cents."

"Apiece?"

"Yes, ma'am."

"Seventy-five cents apiece!"

"I have never received less than that, and some for whom I sew always pay me a dollar."

"Seventy five cents! It is an imposition. I know plenty of poor women who would have been glad of these shirts at half the price - yes, or at a third of the price either. Seventy-five cents, indeed! Oh, no - I will never pay a price like that. I can go to any professed shirt-maker in the city, and get them made for seventy-five cents or a dollar."

"I know you can, ma'am," said Mrs. Walton, stung into self-possession by this unexpected language. "But why should I receive less if my work is as well done?"

"A pretty question, indeed!" retorted Mrs. Lander, thrown off her guard. "A pretty question for you to ask of me! Oh, yes! You can get such prices if you can, but I never pay them to people like you. When I pay seventy-five cents or a dollar apiece for shirts, I go to regular shirt-makers. But this is what we generally get for trying to encourage the poor. Mrs. Brandon said that you were in needy circumstances, and that it would be a charity to give you work. But this is the way it generally turns out."

"What are you willing to pay?" asked the poor woman, choking down her feelings.

"I have had shirts as well made as these for forty cents many and many a time. There is a poor woman down in Southwark, who sews beautifully, who would have caught at the job. She works for the shops, and does not get over twenty-five cents for fine shirts. But as Mrs. Brandon said you were suffering for work, I thought I would throw something in your way. Forty cents is an abundance; but I had made up my mind, under the circumstances, to make it fifty, and that is all I will give. So here is your money - three dollars."

And Mrs. Lander took out her purse, and counted out six half dollars upon the table. Only for a few moments did the poor woman hesitate. Bread she must have for her children; and if her clothes were not taken out of pawn on that day, they would be lost. Slowly did she take up the money while words of stinging rebuke were on her tongue. But she forced herself to keep silence; and even departed, bearing the wrong that had been laid upon her without uttering a word.

"Did you get my shoes as you promised, mother?" eagerly inquired her little boy, as she came in, on returning from the house of Mrs. Lander.

"No, dear," replied the heart-full mother, in a subdued

voice. "I didn't get as much money as I expected."

"When will you buy them, mother?" asked the child as tears filled his eyes. "I can't go to school in this way." And he looked down at his bare feet.

"I know you can't, Harry; and I will try and get them for you in a few days."

The child said no more, but shrunk away with his little heart so full of disappointment, that he could not keep the tears from gushing over his face. The mother's heart was quite as full. Little Harry sat down in a corner to weep in silence, and Mrs. Walton took her sewing into her hands; but the tears so blinded her eyes, that she could not see where to direct the needle. Before she had recovered herself, there was a knock at the door, which was opened immediately afterwards by a lady, who came into the room where the poor widow sat with her little family around her.

More than an hour had passed since the unpleasant interview with the poor widow, and Mrs. Lander had not yet recovered her equanimity of mind nor lost the feelings of indignation which the attempt to impose upon her by an exorbitant charge had occasioned, when she was favoured with a visit from Mrs. Brandon, who said familiarly, and with a smile, as she entered -

"Ah, how do you do, Mrs. Lander? I have just corrected a mistake you made a little while ago."

"Indeed! what is that?" asked Mrs. Lander, looking a little surprised.

"You only gave poor Mrs. Walton fifty cents apiece for the half dozen of shirts she made for you, when the lowest price is seventy-five cents. I always pay a dollar for Mr. Brandon's. The difference is a very important one to her - no less than a dollar and a half. I found her in much trouble about it, and her little boy crying with disappointment at not getting a pair of shoes his mother had promised him as soon as she got the money for the shirts. He has been from school for want of shoes for more than a week. So I took out my purse and gave Mrs. Walton the dollar and a half to make up the sum she had earned, and told her I would see you about it. I acted right, did I not? Of course, it was a mistake on your part?"

Mrs. Lander was never more completely out-generalled in her life. The lady who had corrected her error was one in whose good opinion she had every reason for desiring to stand high. She could grind the face of the poor without pity or shame, but for the world she would not be thought mean by Mrs. Brandon.

"I am very much obliged to you, indeed," she said with a bland smile. "It was altogether a mistake on my part, and I blame the woman exceedingly for not having mentioned it at the time. Heaven knows I am the last person in the world to grind the faces of the poor! Yes, the very last person. Here is the money you paid for me, and I must repeat my thanks for your prompt correction of the error. But I cannot help feeling vexed at the woman."

"We must make many allowances for the poor, Mrs. Lander. They often bear a great deal of wrong without a word of complaint. Some people take advantage of

T.S. Arthur

their need, and, because they are poor, make them work for the merest pittance in the world. I know some persons, and they well off in the world, who always employ the poorest class of people, and this under the pretence of favouring them, but, in reality, that they may get their work done at a cheaper rate than it can be made by people who expect to derive from their labour a comfortable support."

Mrs. Lander was stung to the quick by these words; but she dared not show the least sign of feeling.

"Surely no one professing to be a Christian can do so," said she.

"Yes, people professing to be Christians do these things," was replied; "but of course their profession needs a better practice to prove it of any worth."

When her visitor retired, after having expressed her opinion on the subject under consideration still more unequivocally, Mrs. Lander did not feel very comfortable, nor was her good opinion of herself quite so firm as it had been earlier in the day. But she took good care, in the future, not to give any more work to Mrs. Walton, and was exceedingly particular afterwards, in employing poor people, to know whether they sewed for Mrs. Brandon. There are a good many people in the world who encourage the poor on Mrs. Lander's principle.

JESSIE HAMPTON

"WHAT are you doing here, miss?"

The young girl thus addressed was sitting by a centre-table, upon which stood a lamp, in a handsomely furnished drawing-room. She laid aside the book she was reading, and, without making any reply, rose up quickly and retired. Two or three persons, members of the family, were present. All observed the effect of Mrs. Freeman's words, yet no one had heard what was said; nor would they have been aware that more than a request for some service had been made, but for the lady's remark as the girl left the room.

"I might as well begin at once, and let Jessie know her place."

"What did you say to her, ma?" asked a young lady who sat swinging herself in a large rocking-chair.

"I simply asked her what she was doing here."

"What did she answer?"

"Nothing. The way in which I put the question fully explained my meaning. I am sorry that there should have arisen a necessity for hurting her feelings; but if the girl doesn't know her place, she must be told where it is."

"I don't see that she was doing any great harm," remarked an old gentleman who sat in front of the grate.

"She was not in her place, brother," said Mrs. Freeman, with an air of dignity. "We employ her as a teacher in the family, not as a companion. Her own good sense should have taught her this."

"You wouldn't have us make an equal of Jessie Hampton, would you, uncle Edward?" inquired the young lady who sat in the rocking-chair.

"You cannot make her your equal, Fanny, in point of worldly blessings, for, in this matter, Providence has dealt more hardly with her than with you. As to companionship, I do not see that she is less worthy now than she was a year ago."

"You talk strangely, Edward," said Mrs. Freeman, in a tone of dissent.

"In what way, sister?"

"There has been a very great change in a year. Jessie's family no longer moves in our circle."

"True; but is Jessie any the less worthy to sit in your parlour than she was then?"

"*I* think so, and that must decide the matter," returned Mrs. Freeman, evincing some temper.

The old gentleman said no more; but Fanny remarked -

"I was not in favour of taking Jessie, for I knew how it would be; but Mrs. Carlton recommended her so highly, and said so much in her favour, that no room was left for a refusal. As for Jessie herself, I have no particular objection to her; but the fact of her having once moved in the circle we are in is against her; for it leaves room for her to step beyond her place, as she has already done, and puts upon us the unpleasant necessity of reminding her of her error."

"It don't seem to me," remarked Mr. Freeman, who had till now said nothing, "that Miss Hampton was doing any thing worthy of reproof. She has been well raised, we know; is an educated, refined, and intelligent girl, and, therefore, has nothing about her to create repugnance or to make her presence disagreeable. It would be better, perhaps, if we looked more to what persons are, than to things merely external."

"It is all very well to talk in that way," said Mrs. Freeman. "But Miss Hampton is governess in our family, and it is only right that she should hold to us that relation and keep her place. What she has been, or that she is, beyond the fact of her present position here, is nothing to us."

Mr. Freeman knew from experience, that no particular good would grow out of a prolonged argument on this subject, and so said nothing further, although he could not force from his mind the image of the young girl as she rose up hastily and left the room, nor help thinking how sad a change it would be for one of his own children, if reduced suddenly to her condition.

A good deal more was said by Mrs. Freeman, who did not feel very comfortable, although she fully justified herself for what she had done.

The young girl, who had been reminded so harshly of the error into which she had fallen, went quickly up into her cold chamber, and there, with a burning cheek, sat down to think as calmly as her disturbed feelings would permit. The weakness of tears she did not indulge; self-respect, rather than pride, sustained her. Had she acted from the first impulse, she would have left the house immediately, never again to re-enter it; but reason soon told her that, however strong her impulses might be, duties and considerations far beyond mere feeling must come in to restrain them.

"Whatever I have been," she said to herself, as she sat and reflected, "I am now simply a governess, and must steadily bear that in mind. In this house I am to receive no more consideration than a mere stranger. Have I a right to complain of this? Have I cause to be offended at Mrs. Freeman for reminding me of the fact? Her reproof was unkindly given; but false pride has in it no gentleness, no regard for another's feelings. Ah me! this is one more lesson of the many I have to learn; but let me bear up with a brave heart. There is one who knows my path, and who will see that nothing therein need cause my feet to stumble. From this moment I will think of all here as strangers. I will faithfully do what I have engaged to do, and expect therefor only the compensation agreed upon when I came. Have I a right to expect more?"

The bright colour faded gradually from the flushed cheeks of Jessie Hampton, and with a calm, yet pensive face, she arose and went down into the room which had been set apart for her use when giving instruction to the children. It was warmed and lighted, and had in it a small library. Here she sat alone, reading and thinking, for a couple of hours, and then retired to her chamber for the night.

As was intimated in the conversation that arose upon her leaving the drawing-room, Jessie Hampton's circumstances had suffered, in a very short period, a great change. A year before she was the equal and companion of Fanny Freeman, and more beloved and respected by those who knew her than Fanny was or ever could be; but unexpected reverses came. The relative who had been to her as a father for many years was suddenly deprived of all his worldly goods, and reduced so low as to be in want of the comforts of life. So soon as Jessie saw this, she saw plainly her duty.

"I cannot burden my uncle," said she resolutely to herself. "He has enough, and more than enough, to bear up under, without the addition of my weight." Thoughtfully she looked around her; but still in doubt what to do, she called upon a lady named Mrs. Carlton, who was among the few whose manner towards her had not changed with altered fortune, and frankly opened to her what was in her mind.

"What does your uncle say?" inquired Mrs. Carlton. "Does he approve the step?"

"He knows nothing of my purpose," returned Jessie.

"Then had you not better consult him?"

"He will not hear of it, I am certain; but, for all that, I am resolved to do as I propose. He has lost his property, and is now in great trouble. He is, in fact, struggling hard to keep his head above water: my weight might sink him. But, even if there were no danger of this, so long as I am able to sustain myself, I will not cling to him while he is tossed on the waves of adversity."

"I cannot but highly approve your decision," said Mrs. Carlton, her heart warm with admiration for the right-minded girl. "The fact that your uncle has been compelled to give up his elegant house, and retire with you to a boarding-house, shows the extremity to which he has been reduced. I understand that his fine business is entirely broken up, and that, burdened with debts, he has commenced the world again, a few hundred dollars all his capital in trade, resolved, if health and a sound mind be continued to him, to rise above all his present difficulties."

"And shall I," replied Jessie, "sit an idle witness of the honourable struggle, content to burden him with my support? No! Were I of such a spirit, I would be unworthy the relation I bear him. Much rather would I aid him, were it in my power, by any sacrifice."

"If I understand you aright," said Mrs. Carlton, after thinking for a. few moments, "you would prefer a situation as governess in a private family."

"Yes; that would suit me best."

"How would you like to take charge of Mrs. Freeman's younger children? She mentioned to me, only yester-day, her wish to obtain a suitable instructor for them, and said she was willing to pay a liberal salary to a person who gave entire satisfaction."

Jessie's face became thoughtful.

"Mrs. Freeman is not the most agreeable person to be found, I know, Jessie," said her friend; "but the step you propose involves sacrifices from the beginning."

"It does, I know; and I must not forget this. Had I a choice, I certainly should not select the family of Mrs. Freeman as the one in which to begin the new life I am about entering upon. She and Fanny are among the few who have ceased to notice me, except with great coldness, since my uncle's misfortunes. But I will not think of this. If they will take me, I will go even into their house, and assume the humble duties of a governess."

Mrs. Carlton immediately called upon Mrs. Freeman, and mentioned Jessie. Some objection was made on the score of her being, an old acquaintance, who would expect more notice than one in her position was entitled to receive. This, however, was overruled by Mrs. Carlton, and, after an interview with Jessie, an engagement was entered into for a year, at a salary of four hundred dollars.

When Jessie mentioned the subject to her uncle, Mr. Hartman, he became a good deal excited, and said that she should do no such thing. But Jessie remained firm, and her uncle was at last compelled, though with great reluctance, to consent to what she proposed, regarding it only as a temporary measure.

The first day's experience of Jessie under the roof of Mrs. Freeman is known to the reader. It was a painful experience, but she bore it in the right spirit. After that, she was careful to confine herself to the part of the house assigned her as a servant and inferior, and never ventured upon the least familiarity with any one. Her

T.S. Arthur

duty to the children who were committed to her charge was faithfully performed, and she received, regularly, her wages, according to contract, and there the relation between her and this family ceased. Day after day, week after week, and month after month, did Jessie Hampton, uncheered by an approving smile or friendly word, discharge her duties. But she had within, to sustain her, a consciousness that she was doing right, and a firm trust in an all-wise and merciful Providence.

Mrs. Carlton remained her steady friend, and Jessie spent an evening at her house almost every week, and frequently met there many of her old acquaintances. Of her treatment in the house of Mrs. Freeman she never spoke, and when questioned on the subject avoided giving a direct answer.

Mr. Hartman's struggle proved to be a hard one. Harassed by claims that he could not pay off at once, his credit almost entirely gone, and the capital upon which he was doing business limited to a few hundred dollars, he found it almost impossible to make any headway. In a year from the time Jessie had relieved him from the burden of her support, so far from being encouraged by the result of his efforts, he felt like abandoning all as hopeless. There are always those who are ready to give small credits to a man whom they believe to be honest, even though once unfortunate in business; but for such favours Mr. Hartman could not have kept up thus far. Now the difficulty was to pay the few notes given as they matured.

A note of five hundred dollars was to fall due on the next day, and Mr. Hartman found himself with but a hundred dollars to meet it. The firm from which he had bought the goods for which the note was given had trusted him when others refused credit to the amount of a single dollar, and had it in their power to forward his interests very greatly if he was punctual in his payments. It was the first bill of goods they had sold him, and Hartman could not go to them for assistance in lifting the note, for that would effectually cut off all hope of further credit. He could not borrow, for there was no one to lend him money. There was a time when he could have borrowed thousands on his word; but now he knew that it would be folly to ask for even hundreds.

In a state of deep discouragement, he left his store in the evening and went home. After tea, while sitting alone, Jessie, who came to see him often, tapped at his door.

"Are you not well?" she asked, with much concern, as soon as the smile with which he greeted her faded from his face, and she saw its drooping expression.

"Yes, dear," he replied, trying to arouse himself and appear cheerful; but the effort was in vain.

"Indeed, uncle, you are not well," remarked Jessie, breaking in upon a longer period of silent abstraction into which Mr. Hartman had fallen, after in vain trying to converse cheerfully with his niece.

"I am well enough in body, Jessie; but my mind is a little anxious just now," he replied.

"Isn't your business coming out as well as you expected?" inquired the affectionate girl.

"I am sorry to say that it is not," returned Mr. Hartman. "In fact, I see but little hope of succeeding. I have no capital, and the little credit I possess is likely to be destroyed through my inability to sustain it. I certainly did anticipate a better reward for my efforts, and am the more disappointed at this result. To think that, for the want of three or four hundred dollars, the struggle of a whole year must prove in vain! As yet, even that small sum I cannot command."

The face of Jessie flushed instantly, as her uncle uttered the last two sentences.

"And will so small an amount as three or four hundred dollars save you from what you fear?" she asked, in a trembling voice.

"Yes, even so small an amount as that. But the sum might as well be thousands. I cannot command it."

"You can, uncle!" replied Jessie, with a glow of exultation on her cheek, and a spirit of joy in her voice. "*I* have the money. Oh! it is the happiest hour of my life!"

And sinking forward, she laid her now weeping face upon the breast of her uncle. Her tears were the out-gushing waters of gladness.

"*You* have the money, child?" said Mr. Hartman, after the lapse of a few moments. "Where did you get it?"

"I have had no need to spend my salary."

"Your salary! Have you saved it all?"

"Every dollar. I had clothing sufficient, and there was no other want to take it from me. Dear uncle, how happy it makes me to think that I have it in my power to aid you! Would that the sum was tens of thousands!"

Mr. Hartman, as soon as the first surprise was over, said, with evident emotion -

"Jessie, I cannot express how much this incident has affected me. But, deeply grateful to you as I feel for such an evidence of your love, I must push back the hand that would force this aid upon me. I will not be unjust to you. I will not take your hard earnings to run the risk of losing them."

A shadow passed over the face of Jessie, and her voice was touched with something like grief as she replied -

"How can you speak to me thus, uncle? How can you push back my hand when, in love, it seeks to smooth the pillow upon which your troubled head is resting? Would you deny me a higher gratification than I have ever known? No - no - you cannot!"

Mr. Hartman was bewildered. He felt as if it would be a kind of sacrilege to take the money of his niece, yet how couldhe positively refuse to do so? Apart from the necessity of his circumstances, there was the cruelty of doing violence to the generous love that had so freely tendered relief. In the end, all objections had to yield, and Mr. Hartman was saved from a second disaster, which would have entirely prostrated him, by the money that Jessie had earned and saved.

A short time after the occurrence of this circumstance, the Freemans gave a large party. Mrs. Carlton, who was present, said to Mrs. Freeman, an hour after the company had assembled -

"Where is Miss Hampton? I've been looking for her all the evening. Isn't she well?"

"What Miss Hampton do you mean?" asked Mrs. Freeman, drawing herself up with an air cold and dignified.

"Miss Jessie Hampton," replied Mrs. Carlton.

"Sure enough!" said a young man, who was sitting by, and who had been attentive to Fanny Freeman; "where is Miss Hampton? I haven't seen her for a long time. What can have become of her? Is she dead, or is she married?"

"Her uncle, I suppose you know, failed in business, and has become poor," replied Mrs. Carlton.

"True. I was perfectly aware of that, but didn't reflect that poverty was a social crime. And is it possible that so lovely a girl as Jessie Hampton has been excluded from the circle she so graced with her presence, because of this change in her uncle's circumstances?"

"It is true to a very great extent, Mr. Edgar," returned Mrs. Carlton, "though I am glad to say that there are a few who can appreciate the real gold of her character, and who love her as truly and esteem her as highly as ever they did."

"A worthy few, and if I were only so fortunate as to fall in company with her, I would be of the number. Is she here to-night?"

The young man looked at Mrs. Freeman, and became aware, from the expression of her face, that the subject was disagreeable to her. With easy politeness he changed the theme of conversation; but as soon as opportunity offered, sought out Mrs. Carlton, and asked a question or two more about Jessie.

"What has become of Miss Hampton? I should really like to know," he said.

Mrs. Carlton could only reply direct, and she answered,

"She is living in this family in the capacity of governess."

"Indeed! I have been visiting here, off and on, for a twelvemonth, but have neither seen her nor heard her name mentioned. Are you sure?"

"Oh yes. I procured her the situation over a year ago, and see her almost every week."

"This being the case, and it also being plain that her worth is not appreciated here, our remarks a little while ago could not have been very pleasant to the ears of Mrs. Freeman."

"I presume not," was returned.

The young man became thoughtful, and, in a little while, withdrew from the crowded rooms and left the house. He was the son of a wealthy merchant, and had recently come into his father's business as a partner. It was to the firm of Edgar & Son that the note of Mr. Hartman, which Jessie had aided him to lift, had

T.S. Arthur

been due.

On the day succeeding the party at Mrs. Freeman's, Mr. Hartman came in to purchase some goods, and, after selecting them, asked if he could have the usual credit.

"Certainly," replied old Mr. Edgar; "and to double the amount of the bill."

Hartman thanked the merchant, and retired.

"You know the five hundred dollar note that he paid last week?" said Mr. Edgar, speaking to his son, and alluding to Hartman, who had just left.

"I do."

"Well, I heard something about that note this morning that really touched my feelings. Hartman spoke of the circumstances to a friend, and that friend - betraying, I think, the confidence reposed in him - related it to me, not knowing that we were the parties to which the note had been paid. On that note he came near failing again."

"Indeed! And yet you have just sold him freely!"

"I have. But such are my feelings that I would risk five thousand dollars to keep him up. I know him to be a man of strict honesty."

"There is no doubt of that," replied the son.

"You remember his niece, I suppose?" said old Mr. Edgar.

"Oh, very well."

"When Mr. Hartman's circumstances became reduced, she, of her own free choice, relieved him of the burden of her support, and assumed the arduous and toilsome duties of a governess in one of our wealthy families, where she has ever since been. On the evening before the note of which I spoke was due, she called to see her uncle, and found him in trouble. For some time he concealed the cause but so earnest was she in her affectionate entreaties to know why he was unhappy, that he told her the reason. He was again embarrassed in his business, and, for want of a few hundred dollars, which one, circumstanced as he was, could not borrow, was in danger of being again broken up. To his astonishment, Jessie announced the fact that she had the sum he wanted, saved from her salary as governess. He at first refused to take it, but she would listen to no denial."

"Noble girl!" exclaimed the young man.

"She must be one in a thousand," said Mr. Edgar.

"She is one in ten thousand!" replied the son, enthusiastically. "And yet worth like hers is passed over for the tinsel of wealth. Do you know in whose family she is governess?"

"I do not."

"I can tell you. She is in the family of Mr. Freeman."

"Ah!"

"Yes. You know they gave a party last night?"

T.S. Arthur

"I do."

"Miss Hampton was not present."

"As much as might have been inferred."

"And yet there was no young lady in the room her equal in all that goes to make up the character of a lovely woman."

"Well, my son," replied the old gentleman, "all I have to say is, that I look upon this young lady as possessing excellencies of character far outweighing all the endowments of wealth. Money! It may take to itself wings in a day; but virtue like hers is as abiding as eternity. If your heart is not otherwise interested, and you feel so inclined, win her if you can. Another like her may never cross your path. With such a woman as your wife, you need not tremble at the word adversity."

The young man did not reply. What his thoughts were, his actions subsequently attested.

After the party, to the distant coldness with which Mrs. Freeman had treated Jessie since she came into her house, were added certain signs of dislike, quickly perceived by the maiden. In addressing her, Mrs. Freeman exhibited, at times, a superciliousness that was particularly offensive. But Jessie checked the indignant feelings that arose in her bosom, and, in conscious rectitude of character, went on faithfully discharging her duties. Since the timely aid she had been able to bring her uncle, she had a new motive for effort, and went through her daily task with a more cheerful spirit.

One day, about six months after the occurrence of the party which has been mentioned, Jessie, a little to the surprise of Mrs. Freeman, gave that lady notice that, at a certain time not far off, she would terminate her engagement with her. The only reason she gave was, that the necessity which took her from home no longer remained. At the time mentioned, Jessie left, although Mrs. Freeman, urged by other members of the family, who could better appreciate the young lady's worth, offered a considerable increase of salary as an inducement to remain.

"What do you think?" exclaimed Fanny, about three weeks subsequently, throwing open the parlour door, where the family had assembled just before tea. "Jessie Hampton's married!"

"What!" ejaculated Mrs. Freeman. "Married?"

"Oh yes, sure enough," said Mr. Freeman, "I heard of it a little while before I left my counting-room. And, more surprising still, she is married to young Edgar."

"Oh, no!" responded Mrs. Freeman, incredulously. "It's some mistake. Never! It cannot be."

"Oh, but it is a fact, mother," said Fanny, with ill-concealed chagrin. "Lizzy Martin was her bridesmaid. They were married at Mrs. Carlton's this morning, and the whole bridal party has gone off to Saratoga."

"He's got a good wife," remarked the brother of Mrs. Freeman, in his quiet way. "I always liked that young man, and like him better than ever now. I knew he was a fellow of good sense; but he has showed himself to possess more of that sterling material than I thought."

Mr. Freeman also gave his opinion, and in doing so, expressed himself pretty freely in regard to the treatment Jessie had received, while in the house.

As for his wife, when the truth assumed an undoubted form, she sunk into mortified silence, and Fanny felt even worse than her mother, and for reasons that lay nearer her heart.

In a little while the bride took her old place in society, and many who, in her seclusion, passed her coldly, or all unnoticed, met her now with smiles and with warm congratulations. Of all the changes that followed as a consequence of her marriage, there was none that filled her with so much delight as the improved prospects of her. uncle, Mr. Hartman. Her husband became his fast friend, and sustained him through every difficulty. One home held them both. How purely and brightly the stream of Jessie's happiness flowed on, need not be told.

Virtue and integrity of character had met their just reward. In adversity she was not cast down, and when prosperity again smiled she was not unduly elated. In either relation to society, she was a dispenser of blessings to those she loved.

It is a fact worthy of notice, that those who looked down upon Jessie, and passed her unnoticed while she was only a governess, now referred to the noble, self-sacrificing spirit that prompted her to act as she had done, and spoke of her conduct with admiration.

THE NEW YEAR'S GIFT

"JUST four weeks off," said a little boy, striking his hands together, "and papa will be home!"

"Yes, four weeks more, and we shall see dear father. It will be the happiest New Year's day we ever had; won't it, mother?" said the little boy's sister, a bright smile playing over her face.

"I hope so," replied the mother. "Father has been away so long, his coming home would make any day in the year a happy one."

"I wonder what he will bring me for a New Year's present?" said the boy.

"I know what I'll get," said the little sister.

"What?"

"A hundred kisses."

"Oh! I don't care much for kisses."

"But I do; and I'm sure of getting them."

"I wonder what mamma will get?"

T.S. Arthur

"I know!" replied the sister, with an arch smile.

"What?"

"Just what I will." And the little girl looked at her mother, and smiled still more archly.

"A hundred kisses, you mean?"

"We'll see."

The mother's hand rested from her work, and she looked at her children, with a calm, yet happy face. Their words had caused her to realize, in imagination, with more than usual distinctness, the fact of her husband's return, which he had written would be on the first day of the coming new year. He had been away for many months, and home had hardly seemed like home during his absence.

"We mustn't think too much about it," said the mother, "or we will get so impatient for dear father's return as to make ourselves unhappy. I am sure we will all love him better than ever we did, when he does come home!"

"I am sure I will," returned the little girl.

"Oh! I think I never loved him so well in my life as I have since he has been away."

Thus talked the mother and her children of the return of one whose presence was so dear to them all.

This brief conversation took place in a farm-house. In the room sat, near the fire, a man whose appearance was any thing but pleasant to the eyes. He was a labourer, who had been hired, some months previously, by the farmer. He did not seem to hear what was said, yet he was listening with reluctant attention. The mother and her children continued still to talk of what was uppermost in their minds - the absent one, and his expected return - until the man became restless, and at last got up and went out.

"I don't wonder Mr. Foster went out of the room," said the boy, as the person alluded to shut the door.

"Why, Edward?" asked his sister.

"Can't you think, Maggy?"

"No. What made him go out?"

"Because we said we were so glad papa was coming home on New Year's day. I'm sure he must have thought of his home. They won't be so glad to see him on New Year's day, as we are to see our dear, good father."

"Why do you say that, my son?" asked the mother.

"I'm sure they can't be so glad," said Edward. "I know I wouldn't be so glad to see my father, if he was like Mr. Foster. Doesn't he spend nearly all the money he gets in liquor? I've heard you say that his poor wife and children hardly have enough to eat or to wear, although he gets very good wages, and could make them comfortable if he would. No, I'm sure they can't love him as we love our father, nor be as glad to see him come home as we will be to see our father. And he knows it, and that made him go out of the room. He didn't like to hear us talking."

The boy was correct in his conclusions. The man Foster, of whom he spoke, did feel troubled. He had children and a wife, and he was absent from them, and had been absent for many months. On New Year's day he was to go home; but many painful feelings mingled with the thought of seeing his long-neglected and much-abused family. Since he had been away, he had expended more than half his earnings upon himself, and yet his appearance was worse than when he went from home, for, in exchange for his money, he had received only poison.

It was evening. Without, the air was cold. The sky was clear, and the moon and stars shone brightly. Foster walked a short distance from the house, trying to drive from his mind the images that had been conjured up by the words of the children and their mother; but he could not. His own abused wife and neglected little ones were before him, in their comfortless home, poorly clad, and pale and thin from want of healthy and sufficient food. Did they think of him, and talk with so much delight of his return? Alas! no. He brought no sunshine to their cheerless abode.

"Wretch! wretch!" he said to himself, striking his hand hard against his bosom. "A curse to them! - a curse to myself!"

For an hour the unhappy man stayed out in the chilly air; but he did not feel the cold. Then he re-entered the house, but did not go into the room where the happy mother sat with her children, but to the lonely attic where he slept.

Twenty miles away lived the wife and three children of Foster. The oldest boy was eleven years of age, and the youngest child, a little girl, just five. Three small mounds, in a burying-ground near by where the humble dwelling stood, marked the place where as many more slept - more blessed than the living. The mother of these children was a pale-faced woman, with a bent forth and an aspect of suffering. She had been long acquainted with sorrow and trouble. Like hundreds and thousands of others in our land, she had left, years before, the pleasant home of her girlhood, to be the loving companion of one on whose solemnly pledged faith she relied with the most unwavering confidence. And, for a time, the trust was not in vain. The first golden period of her married life was a happy time indeed! None could have been more thoughtful of her comfort, nor more tender of her feelings, than was her husband. But, alas! it was with him as with hundreds and thousands of others. Not once did it cross his mind that there was danger to him in the pleasant glass that was daily taken. The bare suggestion he would have repelled as an insult. On the day of his marriage, Henry Foster received from the father of his wife the title-deeds of a snug little place containing thirty acres, which was well stocked for a small farmer. He had, himself, laid by a few hundred dollars. Thus he had a fair start in the world, and a most comfortable assurance of happiness and prosperity. For several years every thing went on pleasantly. The farm was a very garden spot, and had increased from thirty to sixty acres by the purchase of contiguous lands. Then a change became apparent. Foster took more interest than formerly in what was going on in the village near by. He attended the various political meetings held at the "Travellers' Rest," and was a prominent man on training and election days. After a while, his wife

T.S. Arthur

began to look on these days with a troubled feeling, for they generally sent him home in a sad plight; and it took nearly a week for him to get settled down again to his work. Thus the declension began, and its progress was too sadly apparent to the eyes of Mrs. Foster, even before others, less interested than herself, observed it. At the end of ten years from the happy wedding day, the farm, now more like a wilderness than a beautiful garden, was seized and sold for debt. There were no friends to step in and go Foster's security, and thus save his property from sacrifice. The father of his wife was dead, and his own friends, even if they had not lost confidence in him, were unable to render any assistance.

The rented farm upon which Foster went with his family, after being sold out, was cultivated with no more industry than his own had been of late years. The man had lost all ambition, and was yielding himself a slave to the all-degrading appetite for drink. At first, his wife opposed a gentle remonstrance; but he became impatient and angry at a word, and she shrank back into herself, choosing rather to bear silently the ills of poverty and degradation, which she saw were rapidly approaching, than to run the risk of having unkindness, from one so tenderly loved, added thereto.

Affliction came with trouble. Death took from the mother's arms, in a single year, three children. The loss of one was accompanied by a most painful, yet deeply warning circumstance. The father came home from the village one evening, after having taken a larger quantity of liquor than usual. While the mother was preparing supper, he took the babe that lay fretting in the cradle, and hushed its frettings in his arms. While holding it, overcome with what he had been drinking, he fell asleep, and the infant rolled upon the floor, striking its head first. It awoke and screamed for a minute or two, and then sank into a heavy slumber, and did not awake until the next morning. Then it was so sick, that a physician had to be called. In a week it died of brain fever, occasioned, the doctor said, by the fall.

For a whole month not a drop of liquor passed the lips of the rebuked and penitent father. Even in that short time the desert places of home began to put forth leaves, and to give promise of sweet buds and blossoms; and the grieving mother felt that out of this great sorrow was to come forth joy. Alas! that even a hope so full of sadness should be doomed to disappointment. In a moment of temptation her husband fell, and fell into a lower deep. Then, with more rapid steps the downward road was traversed. Five more years of sorrow sufficed to do the work of suffering and degradation. There was another seizure for debt, and the remnant of stock, with nearly all their furniture, was taken and sold. The rented farm had to be given up; with this, the hope of gaining even sufficient food for her little ones died in the wretched mother's mind.

From a farmer on his own account, Foster now became a mere farm labourer; with wages sufficient, however, to have made things comfortable at home under the management of his frugal, industrious wife, if all he earned had been brought home to her. But at least one third, and finally one half, and sometimes more, went to swell the gain of the tavern-keeper. Had it not been that a cow and a few chickens were left to them at the last seizure of their things, pinching hunger would have entered the comfortless home where the mother hid herself with her children.

T.S. Arthur

At last Foster became so good for nothing, that he could not obtain employment as a farm hand anywhere in the neighbourhood, and was obliged to go off to a distance to get work. This, to him, was not felt to be a very great trial, for it removed him from the sight of his half-fed, half-clothed children, and dejected, suffering wife; and he could, therefore spend with more freedom, and fewer touches, of compunction, the greater portion of his earnings in gratifying the inordinate cravings of his vitiated appetite.

Thus, in general, stood affairs at the opening of our story. Let us now take a nearer and more particular view. Let us approach, and enter the cheerless abode of the man who, to feed an evil and debasing appetite, could heartlessly turn away from his faithful wife and dependent little ones, and leave them to the keenest suffering.

New Year's day, to which the farmer's wife and children were looking forward with so much delight, was but little more than a week off, and Mrs. Foster expected her husband home also. But with what different feelings did she anticipate his arrival! He never brought a glad welcome with his presence; although his wife, when he was absent, always looked for and desired his return. He had been away over three months; and was earning twenty dollars a month. But, he had only sent home eighteen dollars during the whole time. This, we need hardly say, was far from enough to meet the wants of his family. Had it not been that George, who was but eleven years old, went every day to a factory in the village and worked from morning until night, thus earning about a dollar and a half a week, and that the mother took in sewing, spinning, washing and ironing, and whatever she could get to do, they must have wanted even enough to eat.

It was but six days to New Year's. Mrs. Foster had been washing nearly the whole day, - work that she was really not able to do, and which always so tired her out, that in the night following she could not sleep from excessive fatigue, - she had been washing nearly all day, and now, after cleaning up the floor, and putting the confused room into a little order, she sat down to finish some work promised by the next morning. It was nearly dark, and she was standing, with her sewing, close up to the window, in order to see more distinctly in the fading light, when there came a loud knock at the door. One of the children opened it, and a man, whose face she knew too well, came in. He was the owner of the poor tenement in which they lived.

"Have you heard from Foster since I was here last?" said the man, with an unpleasant abruptness of manner.

"No sir, I have not," replied Mrs. Foster, in a low, timid voice, for she felt afraid of the man.

"When do you expect him home?"

"He will be here at New Year's."

"Humph! Do you know whether he will bring any money?"

"I am sure I cannot tell; but I hope so."

"He'd better;" - the man spoke in a menacing tone - "for I don't intend waiting any longer for my rent."

No reply was made to this.

"Will you tell your husband, when he returns, my good woman, what I have just said?"

"I will," was meekly replied.

"Very well. If he doesn't come up to the notch then, I shall take my course. It is simple and easy; so you had better be warned in time." And the man walked out as abruptly as he came in. Mrs. Foster looked after him from the window, where she had continued standing, and saw him stop and look attentively at their cow, that stood waiting to be milked, at the door. A faintness came over her heart, for she understood now, better than before, the meaning of his threats.

An hour after dark George came home with his hand in a sling. He went up, quickly, to where his mother was sitting by a table at work, and dropping down in a chair, hid his face in her lap, without speaking, but bursting into tears as he did so.

"Oh George! what is the matter?" exclaimed the mother in great alarm. "What ails your hand?"

"It got mashed in the wheel," replied the boy, sobbing.

"Badly?" asked the mother, turning pale, and feeling sick and faint.

"It's hurt a good deal; but the doctor tied it up, and says it will get well again; but I won't be able to go to work again in a good while."

And the lad, from sobbing, wept bitterly. The mother

leaned her head down upon her boy, and wept with him.

"I don't mind the hurt so much," said George, after he had recovered himself; "but I won't be able to do any thing at the mill until it gets well."

"Can't I go to work in his place, mamma?" spoke up, quickly, little Emma, just in her tenth year. Mrs. Foster kissed the earnest face of her child and said -

"No, dear; you are not old enough."

"I'm nine, and most as big as George. Yes, mamma, I'm big enough. Won't you go and ask them to let me come and work in brother's place till he gets well?"

The mother, her heart almost bursting with many conflicting emotions, drew the child's head down upon her bosom, and held it tightly against her heart.

The time of severer trial was evidently drawing near. Almost the last resource was cut off, in the injury her boy had sustained. She had not looked at his hand, nor did she comprehend the extent of damage it had received. It was enough, and more than enough, that it was badly hurt - so badly, that a physician had been required to dress it. How the mother's heart did ache, as she thought of the pain i her poor boy had suffered, and might yet be doomed to suffer! And yet, amid this pain, came intruding the thought, which she tried to repel as a selfish thought, that he could work no more, and earn no more, for, perhaps, a long, long time.

Yes, the period of severer trial had evidently come. She did not permit herself even to hope that her husband when he returned would bring with him enough money to pay the rent. She knew, too well, that he would not; and she also knew, alas! too well that the man to whose tender mercies they would then be exposed had no bowels of compassion.

Wet with many tears was the pillow upon which the mother's head reposed that night. She was too weary in body and sorrowful in mind to sleep.

On the next morning a deep snow lay upon the ground. To some a sight of the earth's pure white covering was pleasant, and they could look upon the flakes still falling gracefully through the air with a feeling of exhilaration. But they had food and fuel in store - they had warm clothing - they had comfortable homes. There was no fear of cold and hunger with them - no dread of being sent forth, shelterless, in the chilling winter. It was different with Mrs. Foster when she looked from her window at daylight.

George had been restless, and moaned a good deal through the night; but now he slept soundly, and there was a bright flush upon his cheeks. With what a feeling of tenderness and yearning pity did his mother bend over him, and gaze into his fair face, fairer now than it had ever looked to her. But she could not linger long over her sleeping boy.

With the daylight, unrefreshed as she was, came her "never ending, still beginning" toil; and now she felt that she must toil harder and longer, and without hope.

Though little Emma's offer to go and work in the mill in her brother's place had passed from the thought of Mrs. Foster, yet the child had been too much in earnest to forget it herself. Young as she was, the very pressure of circumstances by which she was surrounded had made her comprehend clearly the necessity that existed for George to go and work daily in the mill. She knew that he earned a dollar and a half weekly; and she understood very well, that without this income her mother would be greatly distressed.

After she had eaten her breakfast of bread and milk, the child went up stairs and got an old pair of stockings, which she drew on over her shoes, that had long been so worn as to afford but little protection to her feet; and then taking from a closet an old shawl, drew it over her head. Thus attired, she waited at the head of the stairs until her mother was out of the way, and then went quickly down. She managed to leave the house without being seen by any one, and took her way, through the deep and untracked snow, towards the mill, which was about a quarter of a mile off. The air was bitter cold, and the storm still continued; but the child plodded on, chilled to the very heart, as she soon was, and, at length, almost frozen, reached the mill. The owner had observed her approach from the window, and wondering who she was, or what brought so small a child to the mill through the cold and storm, went down to meet her.

"Bless me! little one!" he said, lifting her from the ground and placing her within the door. "Who are you, and what do you want?"

"I'm George's sister, and I've come to work in his place till he gets well," replied the child, as she stood, with shivering body and chattering teeth, looking up earnestly into the man's face.

T.S. Arthur

"George Foster's sister?"

"Yes, sir. His hand's hurt so he can't work, and I've come to work in his place."

"You have! Who sent you, pray?"

"Nobody sent me."

"Does your mother know about your coming?"

"No, sir."

"Why do you want to work in George's place?"

"If I do, then you'll send mother a dollar and a half every week, won't you?"

The owner of the mill was a kind-hearted man, and this little incident touched his feelings.

"You are not big enough to work in the mill, my child," said he, kindly.

"I'm nine years old," replied Emma, quickly.

"Oh yes! I can work as well as anybody. Do let me come in George's place! Won't you?"

Emma had not been gone very long before she was missed. Her mother had become quite alarmed about her, when she heard sleigh-bells at the door, and, looking out, saw the owner of the mill and her child. Wondering what this could mean, she went out to meet them.

"This little runaway of yours," said the man, in a pleasant voice, "came trudging over to the mill this morning, through the snow, and wanted to take the place of George, who was so badly hurt yesterday, in order that you might get, as she said, a dollar and a half every week."

"Why, Emma!" exclaimed her mother, as she lifted her from the sleigh. "How could you do so? You are not old enough to work in your brother's place."

"Besides," said the man, "there is no need of your doing so; for George shall have his dollar and a half, the same as ever, until he is able to go to work again. So then, my little one, set your heart at rest."

Emma understood this very well, and bounded away into the house to take the good news to her brother, who was as much rejoiced as herself. After inquiring about George, and repeating to Mrs. Foster what he had said to Emma, he told her that he would pay the doctor for attending the lad, so that the accident needn't prove a burden to her.

The heart of Mrs. Foster lifted itself, thankfully, as she went back into the house.

"Don't scold her, mother," said George. "She thought she was doing right."

This appeal, so earnestly made, quite broke down the feelings of Mrs. Foster, and she went quickly into another room, and closing the door after her, sat down by the bedside, and, burying her face in a pillow, suffered her tears to flow freely. Scold the child! She felt more like taking her in her arms, and hugging her passionately to her bosom.

To know that the small income her boy's labour had produced was not to be cut off, proved a great relief to the mind of Mrs. Foster; but, in a little while, her thoughts went back to the landlord's threat and the real distress and hopelessness of their situation. To the period of her husband's return she looked with no feeling of hope; but, rather, with a painful certainty, that his appearance would be the signal for the landlord to put his threat into execution.

Sadly the days went by, each one bringing nearer the time towards which the unhappy woman now looked forward with a feeling of dread. That the landlord would keep his promise, she did not, for an instant, doubt. Without their cow, how could she, with all her exertions, feed her children? No wonder that her heart was troubled.

At last the day before the opening year came.

"Papa will be home to-morrow," said Emma. "I wonder what he will bring me for a New Year's gift."

"I wish he would bring me a book," said George.

"I'd like a pair of new shoes," remarked the little girl, more soberly, looking down at her feet, upon which were tied, with coarse strings, what were called shoes, but hardly retained their semblance. "And mamma wants shoes, too," added the child. "Oh! I wish papa would bring her, for a New Year's gift, a nice new pair of shoes."

The mother heard her children talking, and sighed to

think how vain were all their expectations.

"I wish we had a turkey for father's New Year's dinner," said Emma.

"And some mince pies!" spoke up little Hetty, the youngest, clapping her hands. "Why don't we have mince pies, mamma?" she said, taking hold of her mother's apron and looking up at her.

"Papa likes mince pies, I know; and so do I. Don't you like mince pies, George?"

George, who was old enough to understand better than the rest of them the true cause of the privations they suffered, saw that Hetty's questions had brought tears to his mother's eyes, and, with a thoughtfulness beyond his years, sought to turn the conversation into another channel.

But the words of the children had brought to the mind of Mrs. Foster a memory of other times, - of the many happy New Years she had enjoyed with her husband, their board crowned with the blessings of the year. Her dim eyes turned from her neglected little ones, and fell upon a small ornament that stood upon the mantle. It was the New Year's gift of her husband in better days. It reminded her too strongly of the contrast between that time and the gloomy present. She went quickly from the room, to weep unheard and alone.

New Year's morning at length broke clear and cold. Mrs. Foster was up betimes. It was no holiday to her. Early in the day her husband was to come home, and though she could not help looking and wishing for him to come, yet the thought of him produced a pressure in

T.S. Arthur

her bosom. She felt that his presence would only bring for her heart a deeper shadow.

The children had grown eager for him to come. The younger ones talked of the presents he would bring them, while George thought of a book, yet dared hardly hope to receive one. At last, Emma descried her father far down the road, and announced, in a loud voice, his coming. The heart of the mother throbbed quicker at the word. She went to the window, where the children crowded, feeling troubled, and yet with something of the old gladness about her heart. She strained her eyes to see him, and yet dreaded to fix them upon him too intently, lest more should be seen than she wished to see. He came nearer and nearer, and she was yet at the window, her heart beating audibly. Could her eyes deceive her, or was it indeed so? His form was erect and his step firm, and, though his clothes were the same, they did not look so untidy.

"Thank God!" she ejaculated silently, yet fervently, as he came nearer still - "he is sober."

Yes, he was sober.

"Henry!" she could not say another word, as she took his hand when he came in. Her eyes were full of tears. He pressed her thin, small, labour-worn hand tightly, and then turned and sat down. He, too, was moved as well as she. But the children gathered around him, and seemed gladder to see him than when he was last home. There was a reason for this. Seeing the hand of George in a sling, he inquired the cause, and when told of the accident, appeared deeply grieved, and said he should not go back to the mill any more. The heart of his wife fluttered. Was there a meaning deeper than a momentary impulse? At last little Hetty, who had climbed upon his knee, said, "Where's my New Year's gift, papa?"

The father put his hand in his pocket and pulled out a small picture-book, and gave it to the child who was wild with joy in a moment. He had a larger book for Emma, and Robinson Crusoe for George.

"And what for mother?" asked Emma, looking earnestly at her father. "Haven't you brought dear mother a New Year's gift, too?"

"Oh, yes," replied the father, "I've got something for her also." His voice was a little unsteady as he said this. Then he put his hand into his pocket again, and, after keeping it there for a moment or two, drew out a large folded piece of paper that looked like a title-deed, and handed it to his wife, who took it with a trembling hand. She opened it, read a few words, and, bursting into tears, turned and went quickly from the room. Hers were tears of joy - unutterable joy.

Was it then a title-deed of property that her husband had given her, filling her heart with gladness at the thought of relief from toil, and privation, and suffering? No, it was better than that, and brought a fuller and more perfect joy. It was a *New Year's gift* such as she had never dared hope to receive - the dearest gift in the power of her husband to bestow. Already blotted with tears, it was tightly pressed to her heaving bosom.

What was it? What could it be but the blessed temperance pledge, signed, in a firm hand, with her husband's name.

T.S. Arthur

That was indeed a happy New Year's day to the wife and mother, who, when the morning dawned, felt that she was entering upon the darkest days of her troubled existence. But a brighter day unknown was breaking. It broke, and no gloomy clouds have since arisen to obscure its smiling skies.

AUNT MARY'S PRESERVING KETTLE

"I DECLARE, if these preserves haven't been working!" exclaimed Aunt Mary, as she opened a jar of choice quinces, and perceived that, since they were sealed up and carefully stored for the winter, fermentation had taken place.

"And the peaches, too, as I live!" she added on examining another jar. "Run, Hannah, and bring me my preserving kettle. I shall have to do them all over."

"Mrs. Tompkins borrowed it, you know, yesterday," Hannah replied.

"So she did, I declare! Well, you must run over to Mrs. Tompkins, Hannah, and tell her that I want my preserving kettle."

Hannah departed, and Aunt Mary proceeded to examine jar after jar of her rich store of preserves, and, much to her disappointment, found that all of her quinces and peaches, comprising some eight or ten jars, had commenced working. These she took from their dark corners in the closet, and, placing them on the large table in the kitchen, awaited patiently Hannah's return. In about fifteen minutes her help entered.

"But where is the kettle?" inquired Aunt Mary, eagerly.

"Why, ma'am, Mrs. Tompkins says as how she ain't quite done with it yet; she's finished her pears; but then she has her mamlet to do."

Aunt Mary Pierce was a good woman, and her heart was full of kind feelings towards others. But she had her foibles as well as her neighbours, and among these was an almost passionate admiration of her beautiful bell-metal preserving kettle, which was always kept as bright as a gold eagle. Nothing tried Aunt Mary more than to have to lend her preserving kettle. But as in reading her Bible she found it written - *Of him that would borrow of thee turn thou not away* - she dared not refuse any of the applications that were made for it, and in preserving time these were enough to try the patience of even a better woman than Aunt Mary. The fact was, that Aunt Mary's preserving kettle was the best in the village, and there were at least a dozen or two of her neighbours, who did not think their sweetmeats good for any thing if not prepared in this favourite kettle.

"Ain't it too bad!" ejaculated Aunt Mary, lifting her hands and then letting them fall quickly. "Ain't it too bad! But it is always so! Just when I want my own things, somebody's got them. Go right back, Hannah, and tell Mrs. Tompkins that my preserves are all a working, and that I must have my kettle at once, or they will be ruined."

Hannah started off again, and Aunt Mary stood, far less patiently than before, beside the table on which she had placed her jars, and awaited her return.

"Well," she asked eagerly, as Hannah entered after the lapse of some ten minutes, where is the kettle?"

"Mrs. Tompkins says, ma'am, that she is very sorry that your preserves have commenced working, but that it won't hurt them if they are not done over for three or four days. She says that her mamlet is all ready to put on, and as soon as that is done you shall have the kettle in welcome."

Poor Aunt Mary was, for a few minutes, mute with astonishment. On recovering herself, she did not storm and fret. Indeed, she was never guilty of these little housewife effervescences, usually taking every trouble with a degree of Christian meekness that it would have been well for many in the village, even the minister's wife, to have imitated.

"Well, Hannah," she said, heaving a sigh, "we shall have to wait, I suppose, until Mrs. Tompkins has finished her marmalade. But I am afraid all these preserves will be spoiled. Unless done over immediately on their beginning to work, they get a flavour that is not pleasant. But we must wait patiently."

"It's a downright shame, ma'am, so it is!" said Hannah, "and Iwonder you take it so quietly. If it was my kettle, and I wanted it, I reckon I'd have it too quick. Only just say the word, ma'am, and I will get it for you if I have to take it off of the fire."

"Oh no, no, no, not for the world, Hannah!" replied Aunt Mary, to her indignant help. "We will try and wait for her, though it is a little hard to have one's things always a-going, and never to be able to put your hands on them when you want them."

All the next day Aunt Mary suffered the jars of fermenting preserves to remain on the kitchen table. Every time her eye rested upon them, unkind thoughts would arise in her mind against her neighbour, Mrs. Tompkins, but she used her best efforts to suppress them. About the middle of the next day, as the preserving kettle did not make its appearance, Hannah was again despatched, with directions to urge upon Mrs. Tompkins the pressing necessity there was for its being returned. In due time Hannah made her appearance, but without the kettle.

"Well?" inquired Aunt Mary, in a tone of disappointment.

"Mrs. Tompkins says, ma'am," replied Hannah, "that you needn't be in such a fever about your old preserving kettle, and that it is not at all neigh-hourly to be sending for a thing before it is done with. She says she won't be through with her mamlet before day after to-morrow, and that you can't have the kettle before then."

"Well, it is a downright shame!" said Aunt Mary, with a warmth of manner unusual to her.

"And so I told her," responded Hannah.

"You did! And what did Mrs. Tompkins say?"

"Oh, she fired right up, and said she didn't want any of my imperdence."

"But you oughtn't to have said so, Hannah."

"How could I help it, ma'am, when my blood was

boiling over? It is a shame; that's the truth."

Aunt Mary did not reply, but she thought all that Hannah had said to Mrs. Tompkins, and a good deal more. Indeed, her forbearance was sorely tried. Never since she could recollect, had she felt so unkindly towards any one as she now did towards her neighbour and fellow church member. Often did she try to put away these unkind and troublesome thoughts; but the effort was vain. Mrs. Tompkins had trespassed so far upon her rights, and then put such a face upon it, that she could not help feeling incensed at her conduct.

After a while "day after to-morrow" came, which was on Saturday.

"I must have that kettle to-day, Hannah," said she, and Hannah started off to Mrs. Tompkins.

"You needn't come after that kettle to-day," spoke up Mrs. Tompkins, as Hannah entered, "my marmalade is not all done yet."

"But we must have it to-day, Mrs. Tompkins. Mrs. Pierce says as how I mustn't come home without it. The preserves are nearly ruined now, and all because you didn't send home the kittle when we first wanted it."

"I want none of your impudence," said Mrs. Tompkins, going off at once into a passion, for she was rather a high-tempered woman, "and so just shut up at once. If Mrs. Pierce is so fussy about her old worn-out kettle, she can have it and make the most out of it. A pretty neighbour, indeed! Here, Sally," calling to her help, "empty that kettle and give it to Hannah."

"Where shall I empty it?" asked Sally.

"Empty it into the slop barrel, for what I care; the whole kettle of marmalade will be spoiled any how. A pretty neighbour, indeed!"

Sally, who understood her mistress's mood, knew very well that her orders were not to be literally obeyed. So she took the preserving kettle from the fire, and poured its contents into a large pan, instead of the slop barrel.

"Here's the kettle," said she, bringing it in and handing. it to Hannah. It was black and dirty on the outside, and within all besmeared with the marmalade, for Sally cared not to take the trouble of cleaning it.

"There, take the kettle!" said Mrs. Tompkins in an excited tone, "and tell Mrs. Pierce that it is the last time I'll borrow any thing from her."

Hannah took the kettle, and started for home at full speed.

"So you've got it at last," Said Aunt Mary, when Hannah entered; "and a pretty looking thing it is! Really it is too bad to have a thing sent home in that predicament."

"But ain't she mad though!" remarked Hannah, with something of exultation in her tones.

"What in the world can she be mad about?" asked Aunt Mary in surprise.

"Mad because I would have the kittle. Why, there she had her mamlet on the fire, boiling away, and said you couldn't have the kittle. But I told her you must have it; that your preserves were nearly all spoiled, just because you couldn't get your own kittle. Oh, but didn't she bile over then! And so she told Sally to pour the mamlet into the slop barrel, as it would all be spoiled any how, by your unneighbourly treatment to her."

Poor Aunt Mary was dreadfully grieved at this. She loved the good opinion of her neighbours, and it always gave her pleasure to oblige them; but, in this case, she had been tried beyond endurance. She had little heart now to touch her preserves, and so went off to her chamber and sat down, overcome by painful feelings.

In the mean time, Hannah went to work, and, by dint of half an hour's hard scouring, got the kettle to look something like itself. She then went up and told Aunt Mary that every thing was now ready for doing the preserves over again.

"I reckon we'll not boil them over to-day, Hannah," she replied. "It's Saturday, and you've got a good deal of cleaning to do, and I don't feel much like touching them. The preserves won't get much worse by Monday."

Hannah, who understood her mistress's feelings, and sympathized with her, because she loved her, did not urge the matter, but at once withdrew and left Aunt Mary to her own unpleasant reflections. It so happened that the next day was the Communion Sabbath; and this fact had at once occurred to Aunt Mary when Hannah repeated the words of Mrs. Tompkins, and stated that she was very angry. Mrs. Tompkins was a member and communicant of the same church with her. After sitting thoughtfully in her chamber for some time, Aunt Mary took up the communion service and commenced reading it. When she came to the words, "Ye who do truly and earnestly repent of your sins, *and are in love and charity with your neighbours,*" &c. &c., she paused and sat thoughtful and troubled for some time.

"Am I in love and charity with my neighbours?" she at length asked herself, aloud, drawing a heavy sigh.

"No, I am not," was the mental response. "Mrs. Tompkins is angry with me, and I am sure I do not feel right towards her."

During all that afternoon, Aunt Mary remained in her chamber, in deep communion with herself. For the last twenty years she had never, on a single occasion, stayed away from the Lord's table; but now she felt that she dared not go forward, for she was not in love and charity with her neighbours, and the injunction was explicit. Night came, and at the usual hour she retired, but not to sleep the sweet refreshing sleep that usually locked up her senses. Her thoughts were so active and troubled, that she could not sink away into a quiet slumber until long after midnight. In the morning she felt no better, and, as church time approached, her heart beat more heavily in her bosom. Finally, the nine o'clock bell rang, and every stroke seemed like a knell. At last the hour for assembling came, and Aunt Mary, cast down in heart, repaired to the meeting-house. The pew of Mrs. Tompkins was just in front of Aunt Mary's, but that lady did not turn around and smile and give her hand as usual when she entered. All this Aunt Mary felt.

In due time the services commenced, and regularly progressed to their conclusion, the minister preaching a very close sermon. The solemn and impressive communion service followed, and then the members went up to partake of the sacred emblems. But Aunt Mary did not go up as usual. She could not, for she was not in love and charity with her neighbours. This was noticed by many, and particularly by the minister, who lingered after all had successively approached the table and retired, repeating his invitation, while his eye was fixed upon Aunt Mary.

"What can be the matter?" asked Mrs. Peabody of Mrs. Beebe, the moment she got outside of the church door. "Aunt Mary didn't go up."

"Indeed! It can't be possible?"

"Yes, but it is. For I sat just behind her all the time. She seemed very uneasy, and I thought troubled. She hardly looked up during the sermon, and hurried away, without speaking to any one, as soon as the congregation was dismissed at the close of the communion service. What can be the matter?"

"It is strange, indeed!" responded Mrs. Green, who came up while Mrs. Peabody was speaking.

"I took notice myself that she did not go up."

"I wonder if she has done any thing wrong?"

"Oh, no!"

"Then what can be the matter?"

T.S. Arthur

"I would give any thing to know!"

"Something is wrong, that is certain," remarked one of the little crowd, for the group of two or three had swelled to as many dozens.

Many were the suggestions made in reference to Aunt Mary's conduct; and, before Sabbath evening, there was not one of, the members that did not know and wonder at her strange omission.

After Aunt Mary returned from church, she felt even worse than before. A sacred privilege had been deliberately omitted, and all because she had let unkindness spring up between herself and her neighbour.

"And yet how could I help it?" she argued with herself. "I was tired out of all patience. I only sent for my own, and because I did so, Mrs. Tompkins became offended. I am sure I was not to blame."

"But then," said another voice within her, "you could have gone over on Saturday and made up the matter with her, and then there would have been nothing in the way. One duty neglected only opened the way for another."

There was something in this that could not be gainsaid, and poor Aunt Mary felt as deeply troubled as ever. She did not, as usual, go to the afternoon meeting, for she had no heart to do so. And then, as the shades of evening fell dimly around, she reproached herself for this omission. Poor soul! how sadly did she vex her spirit by self-condemnation.

That evening several of the society called in at the

minister's house, and soon Aunt Mary's singular conduct became the subject of conversation.

"Ain't it strange?" said one. "Such a thing has not occurred for these ten years, to my certain knowledge."

"No, nor for twenty either," remarked the minister.

"She seemed very uneasy during the sermon," said another.

"I thought she did not appear well, as my eye fell upon her occasionally," the minister added. "But she is one of the best of women, and I suppose she is undergoing some sore temptation, out of which she will come as gold tried in the fire."

"I don't know," broke in Mrs. Tompkins, who was among the visitors, "that she is so much better than other people. For my part, I can't say that I ever found her to be any thing extra."

"You do not judge of her kindly, Mrs. Tompkins," said the minister gravely. "I only wish that all my parish were as good as she is. I should feel, in that case, I am sure, far less concern for souls than I do."

Thus rebuked, Mrs. Tompkins contented herself by saying, in an under-tone, to one who sat near her -

"They may say what they please, but I am well enough acquainted with her to know that she is no better than other people."

Thus the conversation and the conjectures went round, while the subject of them sat in solitude and sadness in

T.S. Arthur

her own chamber. Finally, the minister said that he would call in and have some conversation with her on the next day, as he had no doubt that there was some trouble on her mind, and it might be in his power to relieve it.

Monday morning came at last, and Aunt Mary proceeded, though with but little interest in her occupation, to "do over" her preserves. She found them in a state that gave her little hope of being able to restore them to any thing like their original flavour. But the trial must be made, and so she filled her kettle as full as requisite of a particular kind, and hung it over a slow fire. This had hardly been done, when Hannah came in and said -

"As I live, Mrs. Pierce, there is the minister coming up the walk!"

And sure enough, on glancing out, she saw the minister almost at the door-step.

"Bless me!" she exclaimed, and then hurried into her little parlour, to await the knock of her unexpected visitor. At almost any other time, a call from the minister would have been delightful. But now, poor Aunt Mary felt that she would as soon have seen any one else.

The knock came in a moment, and, after a pause, the door was opened.

"How do you do, Aunt Mary? I am very glad to see you," said the minister, extending his hand.

Aunt Mary looked troubled and confused; but she

received him in the best way she could. Still her manner embarrassed them both. After a few leading observations, the minister at length said -

"You seem troubled, Aunt Mary. Can any thing that I might say relieve the pain of mind you evidently feel?"

The tears came into Aunt Mary's eyes, but she could not venture to reply. The minister observed her emotion, and also the meek expression of her countenance.

"Do not vex yourself unnecessarily," he remarked. "If any thing has gone wrong with you, deal frankly with your minister. You know that I am ever ready to counsel and advise."

"I know it," said Aunt Mary, and her voice trembled. "And I need much your kind direction. Yet I hardly know how to tell you my troubles. One thing, however, is certain. I have done wrong. But how to mend that wrong I know not, while there exists an unwillingness on my part to correct it."

"You must shun evil as sin," the minister remarked in a serious tone.

"I know, and it is for that reason I am troubled. I have unkind thoughts, and they are evil, and yet I cannot put these unkind thoughts away."

For a moment the minister sat silent, and then, looking up with a smile, said -

"Come, Aunt Mary, be open and frank. Tell me all the particulars of your troubles, and then I am sure I can help you."

Aunt Mary, in turn, sat silent and thoughtful for a short period, and then, raising her head, she proceeded to relate her troubles. She told him how much she had been tried, year after year, during the preserving season, by the neighbours who had borrowed her preserving kettle. It was the best in the village, and she took a pride in it, but she could have no satisfaction in its possession. It was always going, and never returned in good order. She then frankly related how she had been tried by Mrs. Tompkins, and how nearly all of her preserves were spoiled, because she could not get home her kettle, - how the unkind feelings which had suddenly sprung up between them in consequence had troubled her, and even caused her to abstain, under conscientious scruples, from the communion.

The minister's heart felt lighter in his bosom as she concluded her simple narrative, and, smiling encouragingly, he said - "Don't let it trouble you, Aunt Mary; it will all come right again. You have certainly been treated very badly, and I don't wonder at all that your feelings were tried."

"But what shall I do?" asked Aunt Mary, eagerly. "I feel very much troubled, and am very anxious to have all unkindness done away."

"Do you think you can forgive Mrs. Tompkins?"

"Oh, yes. She has not acted kindly, but I can forgive her from my heart."

"Then you might call over and see her, and explain the whole matter. I am sure all difficulties will end there."

"I will go this day," Aunt Mary said, encouragingly.

The minister sat a short time longer, and then went away. He had no sooner gone, than Aunt Mary put on her things and went directly over to Mrs. Tompkins.

"Good morning, Mrs. Pierce," that lady said, coolly, as her visitor entered. She had always before called Aunt Mary by the familiar name by which she was known in the village.

"Good morning, Mrs. Tompkins. I have come over to say that I am very sorry if I offended you on Saturday. I am sure I did not mean to do so. I only sent for my kettle, and would not have done that, had not some seven or eight jars of preserves been working."

"Oh, it was no offence to send for your kettle," Mrs. Tompkins replied, smiling. "That was all right and proper. I was only a little vexed at your Hannah's impudence. But, Aunt Mary, 'let has-beens be has-beens.' I am sorry that there has occurred the least bit of coolness between us."

Aunt Mary's heart bounded as lightly as if a hundred-pound weight had been taken from it; she was made happy on the instant.

"You don't know how glad I am to hear you say so, Mrs. Tompkins," she said, earnestly. "It has removed a load from my heart. Hereafter, I hope nothing will occur again to disturb our friendly feelings. You may have the kettle again, in a day or two, in welcome, and keep it as long as you please."

The breach was thus easily healed; and had Aunt Mary gone over on Saturday to see Mrs. Tompkins, she would have saved herself a world of trouble.

Still, nothing of this was known to the other members of the church, who were as full of conjecture as ever, touching the singular conduct, as they called it, of Aunt Mary. The minister said nothing, and Mrs. Tompkins, of course, said nothing; and no one ventured to question Aunt Mary.

On the next Sabbath, Aunt Mary came to church as usual, and all eyes were instantly upon her.

Some thought she still looked troubled, and was paler than before, while others perceived that she was really more cheerful. In due time, the minister arose and announced his text:

"Give to him that asketh, and of him that would borrow of thee, turn thou not away."

"My dear friends," said he, on drawing near to the close of his subject, "the text teaches us, besides that of simple alms-giving, the duty of lending; but you will observe, it says not a word about borrowing. Under the law laid down here, we may lend as much as we please, but it gives no license to borrow. Now, as far as I have been able to learn, a number of my congregation have not been very particular on this point. They seem to think that it is helping their neighbours to keep this injunction to lend, by compelling an obedience to the precept, whether they are inclined to obey or not. Now, this is wrong. We are justified in lending to those who need such kind offices, but not to put others to the inconvenience of lending when we are fully able to supply our own wants. This is going beyond the scope of the Divine injunction, and I hold it to be morally wrong to do so. Some of you, I am credibly informed," and his voice fell to a low, distinct, and solemn tone, "are in the habit of regularly borrowing Aunt Mary's preserving kettle - (here Aunt Mary looked up with a bewildered air, while her face coloured deeply, and the whole congregation stared in amazement; but the minister went calmly on) - and this, too, without regard to her convenience. Nor is this all - the kettle is hardly ever returned in a good condition. How thoughtless! how wrong! In this, Aunt Mary alone has been faithful to the precept in my text, while you have departed widely from its true spirit. Let me hope that you will think better of this matter, and wisely resolve to let your past short-comings suffice."

And thus the sermon closed. It may well be supposed that for some days there was something of a stir in the hive. The ladies of the congregation who were among the borrowers of the preserving kettle, and they were not a few, including the minister's wife, were for a time deeply incensed at Aunt Mary, and not a few at the minister. But this temporary indignation soon wore off, for Aunt Mary was so kind and good that no one could feel offended with her for any length of time, more especially where there was really no cause of offence. One by one, they called upon her, as they were enabled to see how really they had been guilty of trespassing upon good nature, and, after apologizing, enjoyed with her a hearty laugh upon the subject. And, finally, the whole thing came to be looked upon as quite an amusing as well as an instructive affair.

After this, Aunt Mary was allowed to possess her beautiful bell-metal preserving kettle in peace, which was to her a source of no small satisfaction. And what was more, in the course of the next preserving season, a stock of twenty or thirty brass, copper, and bell-metal kettles, that had been lying for years on the shelves of a hardware-dealer's store in the village, almost uninquired for, were all sold off, and a new supply obtained from Boston to meet the increased demand.

HOME AT LAST

"WE'RE home at last, and I am so glad!" exclaimed a little girl, not over ten years of age, as she paused at twilight with her mother before a small and mean-looking house, one evening late in the month of November.

The mother did not reply, but lifted the latch, when both passed in. There was no light in the dwelling, and no fire on the hearth. All was cold, dark, and cheerless in that place which had been called "home" by the little girl; yet, cold, dark, and cheerless as it was, she still felt glad to be there once more.

"*I* will get a light, mother," said she, in a cheerful tone, running to a closet, and taking thence a candle and a match.

In a moment or two afterwards the candle was burning brightly, and throwing its light into every corner of that meanly-furnished room, which contained but few articles, and they the simplest that were needed. An old pine table, without leaves, three or four old chairs the paint from which had long since disappeared, a bench and a water bucket, with a few cooking utensils, made up the furniture of the apartment.

A small fire was soon kindled on the hearth, over

T.S. Arthur

which the mother hung a tea-kettle. When this had boiled, and she had drawn some tea, she placed upon the table a few slices of bread and a piece of cheese, which she took from a basket that she had borne on her arm. Then the mother and child sat down to partake of their frugal meal, which both eat with a keen relish.

"I'm so glad to get home again!" the little girl said, glancing up into her mother's face, with a cheerful smile.

The mother looked upon her child with a tender expression, but did not reply. She thought how poor and comfortless that home was which seemed so desirable.

"I don't like to go to Mrs. Walker's," said the child, after the lapse of a few moments.

"Why not, Jane?"

"Because I can't do any thing right there. Amy scolds me if I touch a thing, and John won't let me go any place, except into the kitchen. I'm sure I like home a great deal better, and I wish you would always stay at home, mother."

"I would never go out, Jane, if I could help it," the mother replied, in the effort to make her daughter understand, that she might acquiesce in the necessity. "But you know that we must eat, and have clothes to wear, and pay for the house we live in. I could not get the money to do all this, if I did not go out to work in other people's houses, and then we would be hungry, and cold, and not have any home to come to."

The little girl sighed and remained silent for a few moments. Then she said, in a more cheerful tone,

"I know it's wrong for me to talk as I do, mother, and I'll try not to complain any more. It's a great deal harder for you than it is for me to go into these big people's houses. You have to work so hard, and I have only to sit still in the kitchen. But won't father come home soon? He's been away so long! When he was home we had every thing we wanted, and you didn't have to go out a working."

Tears came into the mother's eyes, and her feelings were so moved, that she could not venture to reply.

"Won't he be home soon, mother?" pursued the child.

"I'm afraid not," the mother at length said, in as calm a voice as she could assume.

"Why not, mother? He's been gone a long time."

"I cannot tell you, my child. But I don't expect him home soon."

"Oh, I wish he would come," the child responded, earnestly. "If he was only home, you would not have to go out to work any more."

The mother thought that she heard the movement of some one near the door, and leant her head in a listening attitude. But all was silent without, save the occasional sound of footsteps as some one hurried by.

To give the incidents and characters that we have introduced their true interest, we must go back some

T.S. Arthur

twelve years, and bring the history of at least one of the individuals down from that time.

A young lady and one of more mature age sat near a window, conversing earnestly, about the period to which we have reference.

"I would make it an insuperable objection," the elder of the two said, in a decided tone.

"But surely there can be no harm in his drinking a glass of wine or brandy now and then. Where is the moral wrong?"

"Do you wish to be a drunkard's wife?"

"No, I would rather be dead."

"Then beware how you become the wife of any man who indulges in even moderate drinking. No man can do so without being in danger. The vilest drunkard that goes staggering past your door, will tell you that once he dreamed not of the danger that lurked in the cup; that, before he suspected evil, a desire too strong for his weak resistance was formed."

"I don't believe, aunt, that there is the slightest danger in the world of Edward Lee. He become a drunkard! How can you dream of such a thing, aunt?"

"I have seen much more of the world than you have, Alice. And I have seen too many as high-minded and as excellent in character as Edward Lee, who have fallen. And I have seen the bright promise of too many girls utterly extinguished, not to tremble for you. I tell you, Alice, that of all the causes of misery that exist in the married life, intemperance is the most fruitful. It involves not only external privations, toil, and disgrace, but that unutterable hopelessness which we feel when looking upon the moral debasement of one we have respected, esteemed, and loved."

"I am sure, aunt, that I will not attempt to gainsay all that. If there is any condition in life that seems to me most deplorable and heart-breaking, it is the condition of a drunkard's wife. But, so far as Edward Lee is concerned, I am sure there does not exist the remotest danger."

"There is always danger where there is indulgence. The man who will drink one glass a day now, will be very apt to drink two glasses in a twelvemonth; and so go on increasing, until his power over himself is gone. Many, very many, do not become drunkards until they are old men; but, sooner or later, in nine cases out of ten, a man who allows himself to drink habitually, I care not how moderately at first, will lose his self-control."

"Still, aunt, I cannot for a moment bring myself to apprehend danger in the case of Edward."

"So have hundreds said before you. So did I once say, Alice. But years of heart-aching misery told how sadly I was mistaken!"

The feelings of Alice were touched by this allusion. She had never before dreamed that her uncle, who died while she was but a little girl, had been a drunkard. Still, nothing that her aunt said caused her to entertain even a momentary doubt of Edward Lee. She felt that he had too much of the power of principle in his character ever to be carried away by the vice of intemperance.

Edward Lee had offered himself in marriage to Alice Liston, and it was on the occasion of her mentioning this to her aunt that the conversation just riven occurred. It had, however, no effect upon the mind of Alice. She loved Edward Lee tenderly, end, therefore, had every confidence in him. They were, consequently, married, and commenced life with prospects bright and flattering. But Edward continued to use intoxicating drinks in moderate quantities every day. And, while the taste for it was forming, he was wholly unconscious of danger. He would as readily have believed himself in danger of murdering his wife, as in danger of becoming a drunkard. He was a young merchant in a good business when married, and able to put his young wife in possession of a beautifully furnished house and all required domestic attendance, so as to leave her but a very small portion of care.

Like the passage of a delightful dream were the first five years of her wedded life. No one was ever happier than she in her married lot, or more unconscious of coming evil. She loved her husband tenderly and deeply, and he was all to her that she could desire. One sweet child blessed their union. At the end of the period named, like the sudden bursting of a fearful tempest from a summer sky, came the illness and death of her aunt, who had been a mother to her from childhood.

Scarcely had her heart begun to recover from this shock, when it was startled by another and more terrible affliction. All at once it became apparent that her husband was losing his self-control. And the conversation that she had held with her aunt about him, years before, came up fresh in her memory, like the echo of a warning voice, now heard, alas! too late. She noticed, with alarm, that he drank largely of brandy at dinner, and was much stupified when he would rise from the table - always retiring and sleeping for an hour before going back to his business. Strange, it seemed to her, that she had never remarked this before. Now, if she had desired it, she could not close her eyes to the terrible truth.

For many weeks she bore with the regular daily occurrence of what has just been alluded to. By that time, her feelings became so excited, that she could keep silence no longer.

"I wouldn't drink any more brandy, Edward," said she, one day at the dinner table; "it does you no good."

"How do you know that it does not?" was the prompt reply, made in a tone that expressed very clearly a rebuke for interfering in a matter that as he thought, did not concern her.

"I cannot think that it does you any good, and it may do you harm," the wife said, hesitatingly, while her eyes grew dim with tears.

"Do me harm! What do you mean, Alice?"

"It does harm, sometimes, you know, Edward?"

"That is, it makes drunkards sometimes. And you are afraid that your husband will become a drunkard! Quite a compliment to him, truly!"

"O, no, no, no, Edward! I am sure you will never be one. But - but - but -"

"But what?"

"There is always danger, you know, Edward."

"Oh yes, of course! And I am going to be a drunken vagabond, if I keep on drinking a glass of brandy at dinner time!"

"Don't talk so, Edward!" said Mrs. Lee, giving way to tears. "You never spoke to me in this way before."

"I know I never did. Nor did my wife ever insinuate before that she thought me in danger of becoming that debased, despised thing, a drunkard!"

"Say no more, Edward, in mercy!" Mrs. Lee responded - "I did not mean to offend you. Pardon me this once, and I will never again allude to the subject."

A sullen silence followed on the part of Lee, who drank frequently during the meal, and seemed to do so more with the evil pleasure of paining his wife than from any other motive. So sadly perverting is the influence of liquor upon some men, when opposed, changing those who are kind and affectionate into cruel and malicious beings.

From that hour Mrs. Lee was a changed woman. She felt that the star of love, which for so many happy years had thrown its rays into the very midst of their fireside circle, had become hidden amid clouds, from which she looked at every moment for the bursting of a desolating storm. And her husband was, likewise, a changed man. His pride and self-love had been wounded, and he could not forgive her who had thus wounded him, even though she were his wife. Whenever he was under the influence of liquor, he would brood over her words, and indulge in bitter thoughts against her because she had presumed to insinuate that there was danger of his becoming a drunkard.

At last he was brought home in a state of drunken insensibility. This humbled him for a time, but did not cause him to abandon the use of intoxicating drinks. And it was not long before he was again in the same condition.

But we cannot linger to trace, step by step, his downward course, nor to describe its effects upon the mind of his wife; but will pass over five years more, and again introduce them to the reader.

How sadly altered is every thing! The large and comfortable house, in an eligible position, has been changed for a small, close, ill-arranged tenement. The elegant furniture has disappeared, and in its place are but few articles, and those old and common. But the saddest change of all is apparent in the face, dress, and air of Mrs. Lee. Her pale, thin, sorrow-stricken countenance - her old and faded garments - her slow, melancholy movements, contrast sadly with what she was a few years before.

A lot of incessant toil is now her portion. Lee has, in consequence of intemperance, causing neglect of business, failed, and had every thing taken from him to pay his debts. For a while after this event, he contributed to the support of his wife and child by acting in the capacity of a clerk. But he soon became so dissipated, that no merchant would employ him, and the entire support of the family fell upon his wife. That was, in the very nature of things, an exceedingly meagre support. Mrs. Lee had never looked forward to such a condition in life, and therefore was entirely unprepared for it. Ordinary sewing was all that she could do, and at this she could make but a small pittance. The little that her husband earned was all expended in the accursed poison that had already ruined himself and beggared his family.

After having suffered every thing to sink to this condition, Lee found so little attractive in the appearance of a heart-broken wife and beggared child, and so much about them to reprove him, that he left them without a word, and went off to a neighbouring city.

How passing strange is the effect of drunkenness upon the mind and character of a man! Is it not wonderful how the tender, affectionate, and provident husband and father can become so changed into a worse than brutal insensibility to all the sacred duties of life? Is it not wonderful how the man, who would, to-day, sacrifice even life itself for the safety of his family - who thinks nothing of toil, early and late, that he may provide for every want, can in a few years forsake them, and leave them to struggle, single-handed, with sickness and poverty? But so it is! Instances of such heartless abandonment are familiar to every one. "Surely," as it has been said, "strong drink is a devil!" For he that comes under its influence is transformed into a worse than brutal nature.

For a time after Lee went away, his wife was enabled,

by sewing, to meet the scanty wants of herself and child. The burden of his support had been removed, and that was something gained. But a severe illness, during which both herself and little Jane suffered much for the want of nourishing food, left her with impaired sight. She could no longer, by sewing, earn the money required to buy food and pay her rent, and was compelled to resort to severe bodily toil to accomplish that end.

From several of the old friends of her better days, she had obtained sewing, and necessity compelled her to resort to them for still humbler employment.

"Good morning, Mrs. Lee! I have been wondering what in the world had become of you," said one of those former friends, a Mrs. Walker, as the poor woman called to see her, after her recovery.

"I have been very sick," replied Mrs. Lee, in a low feeble voice, and her appearance told too plainly the effects of the sickness upon her.

"I'm sorry to hear it. But I am very glad you are out again, for my sewing is all behindhand."

"I'm afraid that I shall not be able to do any more sewing for a good while," said Mrs. Lee, despondingly.

"Indeed! And why not?"

"Because my eyes have become so weak that I can scarcely see."

"Then what do you expect to do? How will you get along, Mrs. Lee?"

"I can hardly tell myself. But I must do something."

"What can you do besides sewing?"

"I don't know of any thing, unless I take in washing."

"Take in washing! You are not fit to stand at the washing tub."

"I know that, ma'am. But when we are driven to it, we can do a great many things, even though we gradually fail under our task."

A pause of a few moments ensued, which was broken by Mrs. Lee.

"Will you not give me your washing to do, Mrs. Walker?" she asked, hesitatingly.

"Why, I don't know about that, Mrs. Lee. I never put my washing out of the house."

"You hire some one in the house, then?"

"Yes, and if you will come for what I pay my present washerwoman, why I suppose I might as well throw it in your way."

"Oh yes, of course I will. How much do you give?"

"I give half a dollar a day. Can you come for that?"

"If you will let me bring my little girl along. I could not leave her alone."

"I don't know about that," replied Mrs. Walker,

musingly. "I have so many children of my own about the house."

"She will not be at all troublesome, ma'am," the poor woman urged.

"Will she be willing to stay in the kitchen?"

"Oh yes, I will keep her there."

"Well, Mrs. Lee, I suppose I might as well engage you. But there is one thing that I wish understood. The person that I hire to help do the washing must scrub up the kitchen after the clothes are all out. Are you willing to do that?"

"Oh yes, ma'am. I will do it," said Mrs. Lee, while her heart sank within her at the idea of performing tasks for which her feeble health and strength seemed altogether insufficient. But she felt that she must put her hands to the work, if she died in the effort to perform it.

Three days afterwards, she entered, as was agreed upon, at half a dollar a day, the kitchen of Mrs. Walker, who had but a few years before been one of her friends and companions.

It is remarkable, how persons of the most delicate constitutions will sometimes bear up under the severest toil, and encounter the most trying privations, and yet not fail, but really appear to gain some degree of strength under the ordeal that it seemed, to all human calculation, must destroy them.

So it was with Mrs. Lee. Although she suffered much

T.S. Arthur

from debility and weariness, occasioned by excessive toil for one all unaccustomed to hard labour, yet she did not, as she feared, sink rapidly under it. By taking in as much washing and ironing as she could do, and going out two days in the week regularly, she managed to procure for herself and child the bare necessaries of life. This she had continued for about two years at the time when first introduced to the reader's attention, as returning with her child to her comfortless home.

The slight movement near her door, which Mrs. Lee had thought to be only an imaginary sound, was a reality. While little Jane spoke of her father, and wondered at his absence, a man, comfortably clad in coarse garments, stood near the door in a listening attitude. Once or twice he laid his hand upon the latch, but each time withdrew it and stood musing in seeming doubt. "Oh, I wish father would come home!" fell upon his ear, in clear, distinct, earnest tones.

He did not hear the low reply, though he listened eagerly. Only for a moment longer did he pause. Then swinging the door open, and stepping in quickly, he said in an earnest voice, "And I have come home at last, my child! - at last, my dear Alice! if you will let me speak to you thus tenderly - never, never again to leave you!"

Poor Mrs. Lee started and turned pale as her husband entered thus abruptly, and all unexpected. But she saw a change in him that was not to be mistaken; and all her former love returned with overwhelming tenderness. Still she restrained herself with a strong effort, and said -

"Edward, how do you come?"

"As a sober man. As a true husband and father, I trust, to my wife and child; to banish sorrow from their hearts, and wipe the tears from their eyes. Will you receive me thus?"

He had but half finished, when Mrs. Lee sprang towards him, and fell sobbing in his outstretched arms. She saw that he was in earnest, she felt that he was in earnest, and once more a, gleam of sunshine fell upon her heart.

Years have passed, and no cloud has yet dimmed the light that then dawned upon the darkness of Mrs. Lee's painful lot. Her husband is fast rising, by industry and intelligence, towards the condition in life which he had previously occupied; and she is beginning again to find herself in congenial associations. May the light of her peaceful home never again grow dim.

T.S. Arthur

GOING HOME

"IT'S nearly a year, now, since I was home," said Lucy Gray to her husband, "and so you must let me go for a few weeks."

They had been married some four or five years, and never had been separated, during that time, for twenty-four hours at a time.

"I thought you called this your home," remarked Gray, looking up, with a mock-serious air.

"I mean my old home," replied Lucy, in a half-affected tone of anger. "Or, to make it plain, I want to go and see father and mother."

"Can't you wait three or four months, until I can go with you?" asked the young husband.

"I want to go now. You said all along that I should go in May."

"I know I did. But I thought I would be able to go with you."

"Well, why can't you go? I am sure you might, if you would."

"No, Lucy, I cannot possibly leave home now. But if you are very anxious to see the old folks, I can put you into the stage, and you will go safe enough. Ellen and I can take care of little Lucy, no doubt. How long a time do you wish to spend with them?"

"About three weeks, or so."

"Very well, Lucy; if you are not afraid to go alone, I will not say a word."

"I am not afraid, dear," said the wife, in a voice changed and softened in its expression. "But are you perfectly willing to let me go, Henry?"

"Oh, certainly," was the reply, although the tone in which the words were uttered had something of reluctance in it. "It would be selfish in me to say, no. Your father and mother will be delighted to receive a visit just now."

"And you think that you and Ellen can get along with little Lucy?"

"Oh yes, very well."

"I should like to go, so much!"

"Go, then, by all means."

"But won't you be very lonesome without me?" suggested Lucy, in whose own bosom a feeling of loneliness was already beginning to be felt at the bare idea of a separation from her husband.

"I can stand it as long as you," was Gray's laughing

reply to this. "And then I shall have our dear little girl."

Lucy laughed in return, but did not feel as happy at the idea of "going home" as she thought she would be, before her husband's consent had been gained. The desire to go, however, remaining strong, it was finally settled that the visit should be paid. So all the preparations were entered upon, and in the course of a week Henry Gray saw his wife take her seat in the stage, with a feeling of regret at parting, which required all his efforts to conceal. As for Lucy, when the moment of separation came, she regretted ever having thought of going without her husband and child; but she was ashamed to let her real feelings be known. So she kept up a show of indifference, all the while that her heart was fluttering. The "good-bye" was finally said, the driver cracked his whip, and off rolled the stage. Gray turned homewards with a dull, lonely feeling, and Lucy drew her veil over her face to conceal the unbidden tears from her fellow-passengers.

That night, poor Mr. Gray slept but little. How could he? His Lucy was absent, and, for the first time, from his side. On the next morning, as he could think of nothing but his wife, he sat down and wrote to her, telling her how lost and lonely he felt, and how much little Lucy missed her, but still to try and enjoy herself, and by all means to write him a letter by return mail.

As for Mrs. Gray, during her journey of two whole days, she cried fully half of the time, and when she got "home" at last, that is, at her father's, she looked the picture of distress, rather than the daughter full of joy at meeting her parents.

Right glad were the old people to see their dear child,

but grieved, at the same time, and a little hurt, too, at her weakness and evident regret at having left her husband, to make them a brief visit. The real pleasure that Lucy felt at once more seeing the aces of her parents, whom she tenderly loved, was lot strong enough to subdue and keep in concealment, except for a very short period at a time, her earning desire again to be with her husband, for whom she never before experienced a feeling of such deep and earnest affection. Several times, during the first day of her visit, did her mother find her in tears, which she would quickly dash aside, and then endeavour to smile and seem cheerful.

The day after her arrival brought her a letter - the first she had ever received from her husband. How precious was every word! How often and often did she read it over, until every line was engraven on her memory! Then she sat down, and spent some two or three hours in replying to it. As she sealed this first epistle to her husband, full of tender expressions, she sighed, as the wish arose in her mind, involuntarily, that she could only go with it its journey to the village of -- .

Long were the hours, and wearily passed, to Henry Gray. It was the sixth day of trial before Lucy's answer came. How dear to his heart was every word of her affectionate epistle! Like her, he went over it so often, that every sentiment was fixed in his mind.

"Two weeks longer! How can I bear it?" he said, rising up, and pacing the floor backwards and forwards, after reading her letter for the tenth time. On the next day, the seventh of his lonely state, Mr. Gray sat down to write again to Lucy. Several times he wrote the words, as he proceeded in the letter - "Come home soon," - but

T.S. Arthur

as often obliterated them. He did not wish to appear over-anxious for her return, on her father's and mother's account, who were much attached to her. But, forgetting this reason for not urging her early return, he had commenced again writing the words, "Come home soon," when a pair of soft hands were suddenly placed over his eyes, by some one who had stolen softly up behind him.

"Guess my name!" said a voice, in feigned tones.

Gray had no need to guess whose were the hands, for a sudden cry of joy from a little toddling thing, told that "Mamma" had come.

How "Mamma" was hugged and kissed all round, need not here be told. That scene was well enough in its place, but would lose its interest in telling. It may be imagined, however, without suffering any particular detriment, by all who have a fancy for such things.

"And father, too!" suddenly exclaimed Mr. Gray, after he had almost smothered his wife with kisses, looking up, with an expression of pleasure and surprise, at an old man who stood looking on, with his good-humoured face covered with smiles.

"Yes. I had to bring the good-for-nothing jade home," replied the old man, advancing and grasping his son-in-law's hand, with a hearty grip. "She did nothing but mope and cry all the while, and I don't care if she never comes to see us again, unless she brings you along to keep her in good-humour."

"And I never intend going alone again," Mrs. Gray said, holding a little chubby girl to her bosom, while she kissed it over and over again, at the same time that she pressed close up to her husband's side.

The old man understood it all. He was not jealous of Lucy's affection, for he knew that she loved him as tenderly as ever. He was too glad to know that she was happy with a husband to whom she was as the apple of his eye. In about three months Lucy made another visit "home." But husband and child were along, this time, and the visit proved a happy one all around. Of course, "father and mother" had their jest and their laugh, and their affectation of jealousy and anger at Lucy for her "childishness," as they termed it, when home in May; but Lucy, though half-vexed at herself for what she called a weakness, nevertheless persevered in saying that she never meant to go anywhere again without Henry. "That was settled."

Choose from Thousands of 1stWorldLibrary Classics By

A. M. Barnard	C. M. Ingleby	Elizabeth Gaskell
Ada Leverson	Carolyn Wells	Elizabeth McCracken
Adolphus William Ward	Catherine Parr Traill	Elizabeth Von Arnim
Aesop	Charles A. Eastman	Ellem Key
Agatha Christie	Charles Amory Beach	Emerson Hough
Alexander Aaronsohn	Charles Dickens	Emilie F. Carlen
Alexander Kielland	Charles Dudley Warner	Emily Dickinson
Alexandre Dumas	Charles Farrar Browne	Enid Bagnold
Alfred Gatty	Charles Ives	Enilor Macartney Lane
Alfred Ollivant	Charles Kingsley	Erasmus W. Jones
Alice Duer Miller	Charles Klein	Ernie Howard Pie
Alice Turner Curtis	Charles Hanson Towne	Ethel May Dell
Alice Dunbar	Charles Lathrop Pack	Ethel Turner
Allen Chapman	Charles Romyn Dake	Ethel Watts Mumford
Ambrose Bierce	Charles Whibley	Eugenie Foa
Amelia E. Barr	Charles Willing Beale	Eugene Wood
Amory H. Bradford	Charlotte M. Braeme	Eustace Hale Ball
Andrew Lang	Charlotte M. Yonge	Evelyn Everett-green
Andrew McFarland Davis	Charlotte Perkins Stetson	Everard Cotes
Andy Adams	Clair W. Hayes	F. H. Cheley
Anna Alice Chapin	Clarence Day Jr.	F. J. Cross
Anna Sewell	Clarence E. Mulford	F. Marion Crawford
Annie Besant	Clemence Housman	Federick Austin Ogg
Annie Hamilton Donnell	Confucius	Ferdinand Ossendowski
Annie Payson Call	Coningsby Dawson	Francis Bacon
Annie Roe Carr	Cornelis DeWitt Wilcox	Francis Darwin
Annonaymous	Cyril Burleigh	Frances Hodgson Burnett
Anton Chekhov	D. H. Lawrence	Frances Parkinson Keyes
Arnold Bennett	Daniel Defoe	Frank Gee Patchin
Arthur Conan Doyle	David Garnett	Frank Harris
Arthur M. Winfield	Dinah Craik	Frank Jewett Mather
Arthur Ransome	Don Carlos Janes	Frank L. Packard
Arthur Schnitzler	Donald Keyhoe	Frank V. Webster
Atticus	Dorothy Kilner	Frederic Stewart Isham
B.H. Baden-Powell	Dougan Clark	Frederick Trevor Hill
B. M. Bower	Douglas Fairbanks	Frederick Winslow Taylor
B. C. Chatterjee	E. Nesbit	Friedrich Kerst
Baroness Emmuska Orczy	E.P.Roe	Friedrich Nietzsche
Baroness Orczy	E. Phillips Oppenheim	Fyodor Dostoyevsky
Basil King	Earl Barnes	G.A. Henty
Bayard Taylor	Edgar Rice Burroughs	G.K. Chesterton
Ben Macomber	Edith Van Dyne	Gabrielle E. Jackson
Bertha Muzzy Bower	Edith Wharton	Garrett P. Serviss
Bjornstjerne Bjornson	Edward Everett Hale	Gaston Leroux
Booth Tarkington	Edward J. O'Biren	George A. Warren
Boyd Cable	Edward S. Ellis	George Ade
Bram Stoker	Edwin L. Arnold	Geroge Bernard Shaw
C. Collodi	Eleanor Atkins	George Durston
C. E. Orr	Eliot Gregory	George Ebers

George Eliot
George Gissing
George MacDonald
George Meredith
George Orwell
George Sylvester Viereck
George Tucker
George W. Cable
George Wharton James
Gertrude Atherton
Gordon Casserly
Grace E. King
Grace Gallatin
Grace Greenwood
Grant Allen
Guillermo A. Sherwell
Gulielma Zollinger
Gustav Flaubert
H. A. Cody
H. B. Irving
H.C. Bailey
H. G. Wells
H. H. Munro
H. Irving Hancock
H. Rider Haggard
H. W. C. Davis
Haldeman Julius
Hall Caine
Hamilton Wright Mabie
Hans Christian Andersen
Harold Avery
Harold McGrath
Harriet Beecher Stowe
Harry Castlemon
Harry Coghill
Harry Houidini
Hayden Carruth
Helent Hunt Jackson
Helen Nicolay
Hendrik Conscience
Hendy David Thoreau
Henri Barbusse
Henrik Ibsen
Henry Adams
Henry Ford
Henry Frost
Henry James
Henry Jones Ford
Henry Seton Merriman
Henry W Longfellow
Herbert A. Giles

Herbert Carter
Herbert N. Casson
Herman Hesse
Hildegard G. Frey
Homer
Honore De Balzac
Horace B. Day
Horace Walpole
Horatio Alger Jr.
Howard Pyle
Howard R. Garis
Hugh Lofting
Hugh Walpole
Humphry Ward
Ian Maclaren
Inez Haynes Gillmore
Irving Bacheller
Isabel Hornibrook
Israel Abrahams
Ivan Turgenev
J.G.Austin
J. Henri Fabre
J. M. Barrie
J. Macdonald Oxley
J. S. Fletcher
J. S. Knowles
J. Storer Clouston
Jack London
Jacob Abbott
James Allen
James Andrews
James Baldwin
James Branch Cabell
James DeMille
James Joyce
James Lane Allen
James Lane Allen
James Oliver Curwood
James Oppenheim
James Otis
James R. Driscoll
Jane Austen
Jane L. Stewart
Janet Aldridge
Jens Peter Jacobsen
Jerome K. Jerome
John Burroughs
John Cournos
John F. Kennedy
John Gay
John Glasworthy

John Habberton
John Joy Bell
John Kendrick Bangs
John Milton
John Philip Sousa
Jonas Lauritz Idemil Lie
Jonathan Swift
Joseph A. Altsheler
Joseph Carey
Joseph Conrad
Joseph E. Badger Jr
Joseph Hergesheimer
Joseph Jacobs
Jules Vernes
Julian Hawthrone
Julie A Lippmann
Justin Huntly McCarthy
Kakuzo Okakura
Kenneth Grahame
Kenneth McGaffey
Kate Langley Bosher
Kate Langley Bosher
Katherine Cecil Thurston
Katherine Stokes
L. A. Abbot
L. T. Meade
L. Frank Baum
Latta Griswold
Laura Dent Crane
Laura Lee Hope
Laurence Housman
Lawrence Beasley
Leo Tolstoy
Leonid Andreyev
Lewis Carroll
Lewis Sperry Chafer
Lilian Bell
Lloyd Osbourne
Louis Hughes
Louis Tracy
Louisa May Alcott
Lucy Fitch Perkins
Lucy Maud Montgomery
Luther Benson
Lydia Miller Middleton
Lyndon Orr
M. Corvus
M. H. Adams
Margaret E. Sangster
Margret Howth
Margaret Vandercook

Margret Penrose
Maria Edgeworth
Maria Thompson Daviess
Mariano Azuela
Marion Polk Angellotti
Mark Overton
Mark Twain
Mary Austin
Mary Catherine Crowley
Mary Cole
Mary Hastings Bradley
Mary Roberts Rinehart
Mary Rowlandson
M. Wollstonecraft Shelley
Maud Lindsay
Max Beerbohm
Myra Kelly
Nathaniel Hawthrone
Nicolo Machiavelli
O. F. Walton
Oscar Wilde
Owen Johnson
P.G. Wodehouse
Paul and Mabel Thorne
Paul G. Tomlinson
Paul Severing
Percy Brebner
Peter B. Kyne
Plato
R. Derby Holmes
R. L. Stevenson
R. S. Ball
Rabindranath Tagore
Rahul Alvares
Ralph Bonehill
Ralph Henry Barbour
Ralph Victor
Ralph Waldo Emmerson
Rene Descartes
Rex Beach

Rex E. Beach
Richard Harding Davis
Richard Jefferies
Richard Le Gallienne
Robert Barr
Robert Frost
Robert Gordon Anderson
Robert L. Drake
Robert Lansing
Robert Lynd
Robert Michael Ballantyne
Robert W. Chambers
Rosa Nouchette Carey
Rudyard Kipling
Samuel B. Allison
Samuel Hopkins Adams
Sarah Bernhardt
Sarah C. Hallowell
Selma Lagerlof
Sherwood Anderson
Sigmund Freud
Standish O'Grady
Stanley Weyman
Stella Benson
Stella M. Francis
Stephen Crane
Stewart Edward White
Stijn Streuvels
Swami Abhedananda
Swami Parmananda
T. S. Ackland
T. S. Arthur
The Princess Der Ling
Thomas A. Janvier
Thomas A Kempis
Thomas Anderton
Thomas Bailey Aldrich
Thomas Bulfinch
Thomas De Quincey
Thomas Dixon

Thomas H. Huxley
Thomas Hardy
Thomas More
Thornton W. Burgess
U. S. Grant
Valentine Williams
Various Authors
Vaughan Kester
Victor Appleton
Victoria Cross
Virginia Woolf
Wadsworth Camp
Walter Camp
Walter Scott
Washington Irving
Wilbur Lawton
Wilkie Collins
Willa Cather
Willard F. Baker
William Dean Howells
William le Queux
W. Makepeace Thackeray
William W. Walter
William Shakespeare
Winston Churchill
Yei Theodora Ozaki
Yogi Ramacharaka
Young E. Allison
Zane Grey